Moving
the Mountain

Women Working for Social Change

WOMEN'S LIVES WOMEN'S WORK

2 $\frac{95}{\pi v}$

Project Staff

SUE DAVIDSON, *Editor*

SHIRLEY FRANK, *Associate Editor*

MERLE FROSCHL, *Field-Testing Coordinator*

FLORENCE HOWE, *Director*

MARY MULROONEY, *Production Associate*

ELIZABETH PHILLIPS, *Editor*

SUSAN TROWBRIDGE, *Design and Production Director*

SANDY WEINBAUM, *Teaching Guide Editor*

Moving the Mountain

Women Working for Social Change

Ellen Cantarow

with Susan Gushee O'Malley
and Sharon Hartman Strom

The Feminist Press
OLD WESTBURY, NEW YORK

The McGraw-Hill Book Company
NEW YORK, ST. LOUIS, SAN FRANCISCO

Photo Research by Flavia Rando

**Library of Congress
Cataloging in Publication Data**

Cantarow, Ellen.
　Moving the mountain.

　(Women's lives/women's work)
　Report of interviews with Florence Luscomb, Ella Baker, and Jessie Lopez De La Cruz.
　Bibliography: p.
　Includes index.
　1. Feminists—United States—Biography. 2. Social reformers—United States—Biography. 3. Women in politics—United States—History. 4. United States—Social conditions—1865–1978. I. O'Malley, Susan, joint author. II. Strom, Sharon, joint author. III. Luscomb, Florence, 1887– IV. Baker, Ella, 1903– V. De La Cruz, Jessie Lopez, 1919– VI. Title. VII. Series.
HQ1412.C36　　301.24′2′0922　　79-11840
ISBN 0–07–020443–8 (McGraw–Hill)
ISBN 0–912670–61–4 (Feminist Press)

Table of Contents

Publisher's Acknowledgments

EARLY IN 1973, Mariam Chamberlain and Terry Saario of the Ford Foundation spent one day visiting The Feminist Press on the campus of the State University of New York/College at Old Westbury. They heard staff members describe the early history of The Feminist Press and its goal—to change the sexist education of girls and boys, women and men, through publishing and other projects. They also heard about those books and projects then in progress; they felt our sense of frustration about how little we were able to do directly for the classroom teacher. Advising us about funding, Terry Saario was provocative. "You need to think of yourselves," she said, "in the manner of language labs, testing and developing new texts for students and new instructional materials for teachers." Our "language" was feminism, our intent to provide alternatives to the sexist texts used in schools. The conception was, in fact, precisely the one on which the Press had been founded.

Out of that 1973 meeting came the idea for the *Women's Lives / Women's Work* project. This project, which would not officially begin for more than two years, has allowed us to extend the original concept of The Feminist Press to a broader audience.

We spent the years from 1973 to 1975 assessing the needs for a publication project, writing a major funding proposal, steering it through two foundations, negotiating with the Webster Division of McGraw-Hill, our co-publisher. We could not have begun this process without the advice and encouragement of Marilyn Levy of the Rockefeller Family Fund from which we received a planning grant in 1973.

For one year, Phyllis Arlow, Marj Britt, Merle Froschl, and Florence Howe surveyed the needs of teachers for books about women, reviewed the sexist bias of widely used history and literature texts, and interviewed editorial staffs of major educational publishers about their intentions to publish material on women. The research accumulated provided a strong case for the grant proposal first submitted to the Ford Foundation in the summer of 1974.

During the winter of 1974–75, Merle Froschl, Florence Howe, Corrine Lucido, and attorney Janice Goodman (for The Feminist Press) negotiated a co-publishing contract with McGraw-Hill. We could not have proceeded without the strong interest of John Rothermich of McGraw-Hill's Webster Division. Our co-publishing agreement gives control over editorial content and design to The Feminist Press; McGraw-Hill is responsible for distribution of the series to the high school audience, while The Feminist Press is responsible for distribution to colleges, bookstores, libraries, and the general public.

In the summer of 1975, the final proposal—to produce for co-publication a series of twelve supplementary books and their accompanying teaching guides—was funded by the Ford Foundation and the Carnegie Corporation. Project officers Terry Saario and Vivien Stewart were supportive and helpful throughout the life of the project. In 1978, The Feminist Press received funds from the National Endowment for the Humanities to help complete the project. Additional funds also were received from the Edward W. Hazen Foundation and from the Rockefeller Family Fund.

Once initial funding was obtained, The Feminist Press began its search for additional staff to work on the project. The small nucleus of existing staff working on the project was expanded as The Feminist Press hired new employees. The *Women's Lives / Women's Work* project staff ultimately included eight people who remained for the duration of the project: Sue Davidson, Shirley Frank, Merle Froschl, Florence Howe, Mary Mulrooney, Elizabeth Phillips, Susan Trowbridge, and Sandy Weinbaum. Two other people, Dora Janeway Odarenko and Michele Russell, were on the staff through 1977, and we wish to acknowledge their contributions. Helen Schrader, a Feminist Press staff member, participated on the project during its first year and kept financial records and wrote financial reports throughout the duration of the project.

The *Women's Lives / Women's Work* project staff adopted the methods of work and the decision-making structure developed by The Feminist Press staff as a whole. As a Press "work committee," the project met weekly to make decisions, review progress, discuss problems. The project staff refined the editorial direction of the project, conceptualized and devised guidelines for the books and teaching guides, and identified prospective authors. When proposals came in, the project staff read and evaluated the submissions, and made decisions regarding them. Similarly, when manuscripts arrived, the project staff read and commented on them. Project staff members took turns drafting memoranda, reports, and other documents. And the design of the series grew out of the discussions and the ideas generated at the project meetings. The books, teaching guides, and other informational materials had the advantage, at significant stages of development, of the committee's collective direction.

Throughout the life of the project, The Feminist Press itself continued to function and grow. Individuals on staff who were not part of the *Women's Lives / Women's Work* project provided support and advice to the project. All major project policy decisions about such matters as finance and personnel were made by The Feminist Press

Board at its monthly meetings. The Board includes all Feminist Press staff, and other individuals who have an ongoing relationship to the Press: Phyllis Arlow, Jeanne Bracken, Brenda Carter, Toni Cerutti, Ranice Crosby, Sue Davidson, Michelina Fitzmaurice, Jeanne Ford, Shirley Frank, Merle Froschl, Barbara Gore, Brett Harvey, Ilene Hertz, Florence Howe, Paul Lauter, Carol Levin, Corrine Lucido, Mary Mulrooney, Ethel J. Phelps, Elizabeth Phillips, Helen Schrader, Merryl Sloane, Susan Trowbridge, Sandy Weinbaum, Sharon Wigutoff, Jane Williamson, Sophie Zimmerman.

The process of evaluation by teachers and students before final publication was as important as the process for developing ideas into books. To this end, we produced testing editions of the books. Field-testing networks were set up throughout the United States in a variety of schools—public, private, inner-city, small town, suburban, and rural—to reach as diverse a student population as possible. We field tested in the following cities, regions, and states: Boston, Massachusetts; Tampa, Florida; Greensboro, North Carolina; Tucson, Arizona; Los Angeles, California; Eugene, Oregon; Seattle, Washington; Shawnee Mission, Kansas; Martha's Vineyard, Massachusetts; New York City; Long Island; New Jersey; Rhode Island; Michigan; Minnesota. We also had an extensive network of educators—350 teachers across the country—who reviewed the books in the series, often using sections of books in classrooms. From teachers' comments, from students' questionnaires, and from tapes of teachers' discussions, we gained valuable information both for revising the book and for developing the teaching guides.

Although there is no easy way to acknowledge the devotion and enthusiasm of hundreds of teachers who willingly volunteered their time and energies, we would like to thank the following teachers— and their students—with whom we worked directly in the testing of *Moving the Mountain: Women Working for Social Change.* In Arizona, Sherry O'Donnell, Acting Chairperson of the Women's Studies Committee at the University of Arizona, and Betty Newlon, Professor of Education at the University of Arizona—with the assistance of Kay Kavanaugh—helped to contact the following teachers in the Tucson area: Mary Lynn Hamilton, Mari Helen High, Dorothy Livieratos, Beverly Middleton-Johnson, Kristin Wallace. We also wish to acknowledge Myra Dinnerstein, Chairperson of the Women's Studies Committee, for her help in the development of the Tucson network. In California, Lilyan Frank in the Department of English at the University of Southern California helped to contact teachers in the Los Angeles area: Sharon Geltner, Helen Kelly, Rhonda Nalisnik, Marion Walker, Ira West. In Eugene, Oregon, Bev

Melugin, Instructional Materials Analyst, and Anne Stewart, Coordinator of Women's Programs at Lane Community College, helped to contact the following teachers: Kate Barry, Yvonne Fasold, Orris L. Goode, Ann Monro, Ronalee Ramsay, Harriet Wilson. In Seattle, Washington, Audra Adelberger of Feminists Northwest and Edith Ruby, Sex Balance Curriculum Consultant to the Seattle public schools, helped to contact the following teachers: Roxie Day, Shirley Dunphy, Sara Kaplan, Suzanna Kline, Nancy Mason, Laurel Ann Pickett. We also wish to acknowledge the participation of Joan Augerot, Eleanor Bilimoria, Larae Glennon, Sharon Greene, Cynthia Lambarth, Ruth Pelz, and Gisela E. Taber.

Three times during the life of the *Women's Lives / Women's Work* project, an Advisory Board composed of feminist educators and scholars met for a full day to discuss the books and teaching guides. The valuable criticisms and suggestions of the following people who participated in these meetings were essential to the project: Millie Alpern, Rosalynn Baxandall, Peggy Brick, Ellen Cantarow, Elizabeth Ewen, Barbara Gates, Clarisse Gillcrist, Elaine Hedges, Nancy Hoffman, Susan Klaw, Alice Kessler-Harris, Roberta Kronberger, Merle Levine, Eleanor Newirth, Judith Oksner, Naomi Rosenthal, Judith Schwartz, Judy Scott, Carroll Smith-Rosenberg, Adria Steinberg, Barbara Sussman, Amy Swerdlow. We also want to express our gratitude to Shirley McCune and Nida Thomas, who acted in a general advisory capacity and made many useful suggestions; and to Kathryn Girard and Kathy Salisbury who helped to develop the teacher and student field-testing questionnaires.

One person in particular whom we wish to thank for her work on *Moving the Mountain* is Flavia Rando for her exhaustive photo research and her unbounded enthusiasm for the job. Indeed, her research unearthed so many excellent photographs that it was with great difficulty that we limited ourselves to the ones that we finally selected for this volume.

Others whom we want to acknowledge are Ruth Adam for restoration of the historical photographs; Judith McQuown who prepared the index; Carlos Ruiz of McGraw-Hill for administrative assistance; and Emerson W. Madairy of Monotype Composition Company for technical assistance.

The work of the many people mentioned in these acknowledgments has been invaluable to us. We would also like to thank all of you who read this book—because you helped to create the demand that made the *Women's Lives / Women's Work* project possible.

THE FEMINIST PRESS

Preface

As I was first thinking about this book, the following verses by the German poet, Bertolt Brecht, kept running through my mind:

> Who built the seven towers of Thebes?
> The books are filled with the names of kings.
> Was it kings who hauled the craggy blocks of stone? . . .
> In the evening when the Chinese wall was finished
> Where did the masons go?

Ordinary people, Brecht is saying, make buildings and history, while presidents, army commanders, and scientific "experts" make news headlines. The stories of the ordinary people get lost: only the buildings and walls bear witness to the labor of the hands that built them.

Moving the Mountain is based on the idea that the stories of people working behind the scenes to build mass movements for social change are indispensable for understanding how social change takes place. The book suggests that behind-the-scenes organizers—especially women—have been as important in such movements as the leaders whose names make the front pages of newspapers. Looking for a number of women who might represent a variety of movements and social backgrounds, I finally settled on three veteran activists: Florence Luscomb, Ella Baker, and Jessie De La Cruz. They are known and loved by the people who have worked with them, but are still unknown by the general public.

Acquaintances and friends told me that Sharon Strom had been working for a long time with a colleague, Steven Halpern, interviewing Luscomb for a biography of the remarkable, ninety-year-old Boston radical. And so I asked Strom to write the Luscomb chapter, on which I have worked only as a co-editor. Susan O'Malley, who lived and worked in the South during the civil rights movement, offered to be my co-interviewer for the chapter on Ella Baker's life, and I accepted with pleasure, since O'Malley knew many people who had worked closely with this "organizer's organizer" in black liberation movements. Deborah Silverton Rosenfelt, editor of The Feminist Press reprint of *Salt of the Earth*, a play about a Mexican American zinc miners' strike, suggested that I interview Jessie De La Cruz, known among United Farmworker members and others as a profoundly effective organizer with a rare combination of qualities—modesty, determination, and eloquence.

Moving the Mountain is a trilogy—three life stories as they were told to Sharon Strom, Susan O'Malley, and me. The process by which the book was written has come to be called "oral history." This is a name only recently given to what is actually a very old process. There was a time when people learned about history through their families, through official poets, singers, and storytellers. The events that were considered important in a community were passed on by word of mouth, not by way of newspapers, textbooks, and other written documents.

Much of the oral tradition has been lost in the United States, although it lives on in such forms as the blues. And, some people have been trying to rebuild the oral tradition. In the 1930s, historians and anthropologists were hired under government programs to interview thousands of people. The resulting narratives give spellbinding information about those incidents in daily life that grip one the most—and that rarely get written up in ordinary textbooks. Among the people interviewed by the oral historians of the thirties were men and women who had been slaves. Their stories have been published in some numbers since the civil rights movement of the 1960s.

There is a democratic idea at the heart of oral history: that the people who have lived through particular events are the ones best qualified to talk about them. This isn't always true (everyone has memory lapses, for instance), but it does offer an alternative to the notion that the only people who can talk with authority about the past and the present are professional scholars, teachers, and news commentators.

An oral history begins with an idea—for instance, the idea of writing a history about three generations of a family. And one must find those people who can best talk about themselves so as to make the overall idea live. For the interviewing, one must come prepared with informed questions. If one is interviewing a relative, one's long relationship with that person will probably provide most of the questions, and extensive research may not be needed. But in other cases, one must become familiar—through reading books, back issues of newspapers, magazines, and the like—with the historical events that surround people's lives. For example, although Susan O'Malley and I knew much about the civil rights movement, we spent a great deal of time poring over material in Harlem's Schomberg Collection—particularly to see whether any contained references to Ella Baker.

Next, the interview itself. Ella Baker allowed us to spend several hours with her the first day, several more on a second visit. It is impossible to produce a life's story out of two days of interviewing, and Ella Baker's chapter does not represent that. Rather, we hoped it would suggest, through a selection of reminiscences, the richness of Baker's life. Oral historians often visit their interviewees over the course of months or even years—as Sharon Strom has with Florence Luscomb. Other interviewers, like Studs Terkel, author of *Hard Times* and *Working,* do very brief interviews in a few hours.

Contemporary oral historians almost always use tape recorders. After an interview, one must transcribe what has been recorded— a long process. The typed transcript represents an enormous quantity of raw material: it is not the final product. One must cut out some sections and shift others around to arrive at a coherent, lively story. Most people, even the most eloquent, go off on tangents. In answering one question, they remember something they want to add to a preceding question. There are many "um's," "well's," and the like. The idea is to cut, splice, and rearrange the original raw material while conveying the interviewee's personality, her way of speaking, as faithfully as possible. It is a little like making a film. To give a very small example of this process, in organizing the entire Baker transcript, I found reminiscences about Baker's childhood near the end of the interview. Naturally, I moved that portion of the interview up to the beginning of the narrative.

A critical part of oral history is the interviewer's own introduction. Since the story is the interviewee's, the introduction should not overwhelm the narrative. But the length of introductory material varies depending on the nature and length of the narrative, and on the purpose of the book. As the three stories here unfolded, it became clear to me that relatively long introductions would be necessary. Not only were the oral histories comparatively long, but the social movements they described were often little known. And so it seemed that background history would be needed if each woman's story was to be fully understandable. I chose to divide the oral histories into short sections, heading each with what I hoped might be minimal prefaces. But many of the original prefaces began growing beyond the one-page limit I had originally set. For instance, as Sharon Strom, Elizabeth Phillips (general editor of the book), and I wrote letters back and forth about the Florence Luscomb manuscript, it became clear that Strom's introduction to the section on the thirties would have to nearly double in length. We believed that by providing more details on the Depression, the labor movement, and the Communist party, we would illuminate Luscomb's participation in social movements of the period.

No one who has done an in-depth oral history has emerged unchanged by the experience. Sharon Strom first invited Florence Luscomb to speak on suffrage in a college history class, then began a long series of interviews with her. Of the friendship that grew between them, Strom wrote, "Florence Luscomb introduced me to a whole past to which I could relate in a special way, both in my teaching and in my own life. I also saw in her a model for my own adulthood and aging. It became clear that being 'political' didn't mean self-sacrifice, but a full, rich life that could extend far into old age." Susan O'Malley and I felt the same kinds of emotions about our much briefer, but deeply affecting, time with Ella Baker. She seemed to us a true "foremother"—an example of strength for our own lives, a single woman on her own in the world, bound to others through her deep political commitments. Moreover, in a country where what one earns and owns continues, increasingly, to define one's "status," Ella Baker reminded us that life is made meaningful, finally, only to the extent that one's friendships are shaped by humane beliefs, not by wealth, titles, or possessions.

Jessie and Arnold De La Cruz literally opened their doors and insisted that I stay with them during the week I spent in Fresno for my interviews with Jessie. The time I spent with the De La Cruzes will always be a vivid, unique part of my life. Their commitment to mutual aid and cooperative work, and their knowledge of the land, rekindled my belief that people like them could better inspire and guide daily life in the United States than many present "leaders." My stay with them gave me a glimpse, not only of the hardship and toil, but of the resilience, understanding, and humor of a people who have been ignored by textbooks and the media alike. I will also remember with great warmth the time I spent in the house of the organization, National Land for People, for which Jessie De La Cruz works, and of the hours in which I came to know George Ballis, Maia Sortor, and the other members of this small but extraordinary group that is fighting some of the biggest corporations in the world.

For this book, I am indebted not only to my co-authors and to the three women who permitted their stories to be told publicly, but to others as well: to my friend and colleague, Florence Howe, who originally suggested the project to me; to my editor, Elizabeth Phillips, always enthusiastic about the stories as they unfolded, and always helpful in her advice; to Phyllis Ewen who gave friendship and support, and who read parts of the book while I was writing it; to Deborah Rosenfelt, who shared knowledge, material, and, while I was in California, her house, and who guided me to others for information for the De La Cruz chapter; to Ann Withorn of *Radical America*, who generously shared parts of her thesis with me as background for sections of the book; to Flora Haas of the *Boston Phoenix*, friend and fellow journalist, who shared with me her encyclopedic knowledge about critical parts of the United Farmworkers campaigns; and to Louis Kampf, who patiently read the chapters as I was writing and editing them. A final note: without the women's studies, Black studies and Chicano studies movements, which have built up rich storehouses of source material, the long task of writing the historical prefaces to the narratives of Baker and De La Cruz would have been impossible.

ELLEN CANTAROW

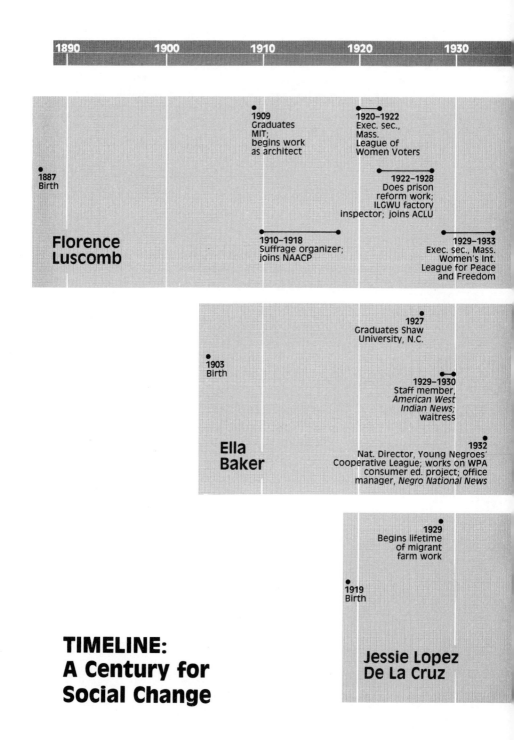

1890 1900 1910 1920 1930

1909
Graduates
MIT;
begins work
as architect

1920–1922
Exec. sec.,
Mass.
League of
Women Voters

●1887
Birth

1922–1928
Does prison
reform work;
ILGWU factory
inspector; joins ACLU

Florence
Luscomb

1910–1918
Suffrage organizer;
joins NAACP

1929–1933
Exec. sec., Mass.
Women's Int.
League for Peace
and Freedom

1927
Graduates Shaw
University, N.C.

●1903
Birth

1929–1930
Staff member,
*American West
Indian News;*
waitress

Ella
Baker

1932
Nat. Director, Young Negroes'
Cooperative League; works on WPA
consumer ed. project; office
manager, *Negro National News*

1929
Begins lifetime
of migrant
farm work

●1919
Birth

Jessie Lopez
De La Cruz

TIMELINE:
A Century for
Social Change

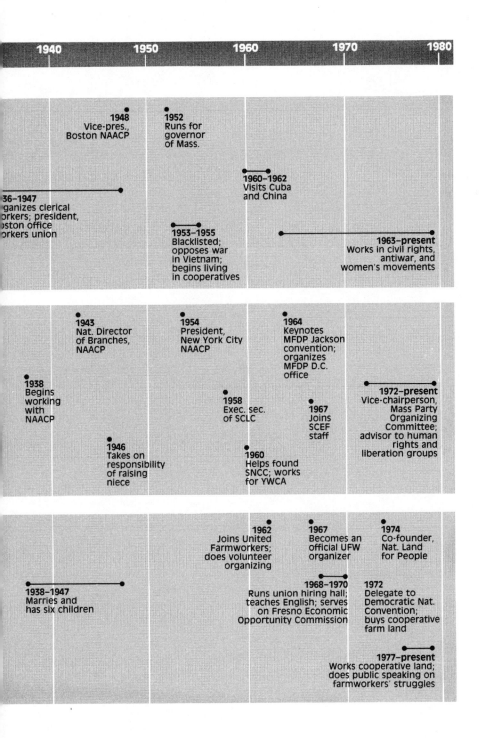

1940 1950 1960 1970 1980

●
1948
Vice-pres.,
Boston NAACP

●
1952
Runs for
governor
of Mass.

●——————●
1960–1962
Visits Cuba
and China

36–1947
ganizes clerical
orkers; president,
oston office
orkers union

●——————●
1953–1955
Blacklisted;
opposes war
in Vietnam;
begins living
in cooperatives

●——————●
1963–present
Works in civil rights,
antiwar, and
women's movements

●
1943
Nat. Director
of Branches,
NAACP

●
1954
President,
New York City
NAACP

●
1964
Keynotes
MFDP Jackson
convention;
organizes
MFDP D.C.
office

●
1938
Begins
working
with
NAACP

●
1958
Exec. sec.
of SCLC

●
1967
Joins
SCEF
staff

●——————●
1972–present
Vice-chairperson,
Mass Party
Organizing
Committee;
advisor to human
rights and
liberation groups

●
1946
Takes on
responsibility
of raising
niece

●
1960
Helps found
SNCC; works
for YWCA

●
1962
Joins United
Farmworkers;
does volunteer
organizing

●
1967
Becomes an
official UFW
organizer

●
1974
Co-founder,
Nat. Land
for People

●——————●
1938–1947
Marries and
has six children

●——————●
1968–1970
Runs union hiring hall;
teaches English; serves
on Fresno Economic
Opportunity Commission

1972
Delegate to
Democratic Nat.
Convention;
buys cooperative
farm land

●——————●
1977–present
Works cooperative land;
does public speaking on
farmworkers' struggles

Introduction

DURING THE SECOND DECADE of this century, my grandmother was an activist. A woman in her thirties, she was part of a feminist movement that was nearly seventy years old. Women active in the drive against slavery had launched a movement for their own rights in the 1840s. In my grandmother's time, the feminist movement was largely intent on getting the right to vote. My grandmother had three children to raise. She had massive piles of laundry to hand wash and ironing to do. She had huge meals to prepare. But her energy was boundless. The movement had sown the irresistible idea of women's equality, and there were organizations to drive forward her energies and ideals.

According to her children, she would descend the front steps of the family's house in Philadelphia, Pennsylvania, bearing a large banner that read VOTES FOR WOMEN, to go out into the streets and march in suffrage parades. That image of my grandmother, going down the steps with the banner rolled up and tucked under her arm, is the only one passed on through the family. Perhaps family members did not disapprove outright of her activism. But they certainly felt it was secondary to her home life. In their eyes, such things were bad enough for anyone to do—still worse for a woman, and worst of all for a married woman with children. What were my grandmother's ideas? How did her passion for justice, which propelled her—an otherwise conventional woman—out of the house and into the streets, come out of her growing up, marriage, and motherhood? What, exactly, did she do between the time she left the house and the time she came home again?

There are no answers to these questions. My grandmother's story lies buried in silence, as do the stories of many women active not only in the suffrage movement, but in labor, civil rights, education, and other movements for social change in the United States. The silence that engulfs their stories is not only the result of family disapproval. Often the families of women like the three in this book were proud of the activism of their grandmothers, mothers, aunts, and sisters. More often, the silence exists because history texts have ignored

women in particular, social activists in general. The writers of
the texts have assumed it is important to learn about "great
men." "Great men" has meant men at the top of the social
heap. Captains of industry. Owners of vast tracts of land. Presidents and senators. Generals. Perhaps one or two labor chiefs.
These men have almost always been white.

The voices of all women; of black, Asian American, His-
panic, Mexican American and Native American women and
men; * of gay women and men; the voices of working people and
the poor—these have not been heard in the pages of the texts.
To be sure, a token woman might surface here and there. A few
sentences might sum up the life's work of Elizabeth Cady Stanton, a major leader of the nineteenth-century feminist movement. A token black man, like the outstanding abolitionist and
orator Frederick Douglass, might get the same brief mention,
although until very recently, black women have rarely gotten
as much as a single sentence. As for Mexican Americans, from
what the textbooks indicate, they might not have existed.

Although many stories like my grandmother's are lost forever, some have recently been rediscovered. Out of the social
movements of the 1960s—the civil rights, antiwar, farmworkers', and women's movements—emerged new ideas about
who was important in history. Seemingly powerless people
shaped these movements. Black students sat down at segregated lunch counters in small southern towns. Women met in
small discussion groups that would swell into the women's
liberation movement of the late sixties and early seventies.
GIs defied their officers in Southeast Asia. Students tore up
draft cards in mass demonstrations in cities throughout the
United States. Welfare mothers occupied local welfare offices.
Mexican American farm laborers tried, for the first time in
years, to unionize. And thousands of miles away, an international backdrop to what was happening at home, a small
country, Vietnam, staved off the greatest military power in the
world, the United States.

---

* Native American is a term used to describe people whites have generally
called Indians. The term derives from the fact that Indians are the only
people truly native to the Americas.

Many people became convinced that the seemingly power-less were, in fact, the makers of history. With that realization came a desire to find out about such people of the past. Women in particular—activists, writers, and teachers working within the women's movement—searched for their lost foremothers. Often, they found them vigorous in their eighties and nineties, living histories of mass movements that stretched from the early suffrage movement to the movement against the Vietnam war.[1]

One such woman is Florence Luscomb, who in this book tells the story of her work in suffrage, labor, and peace movements from the beginning of the twentieth century to the present. Another such woman is Ella Baker, for nearly fifty years an organizer for civil rights and black liberation movements. Still another—younger, driving on in her early sixties toward an old age as active as Luscomb's and Baker's—is Jessie De La Cruz. She was the first woman to organize in the fields for the United Farmworkers. She would later work in a movement of farmworkers to get land of their own. These three women tell the stories of their lives in their own words. Their accounts are called "oral history"—history spoken aloud by the people who have lived it.

Recovering Our Lost Foremothers

Moving the Mountain begins filling in my grandmother's day by telling about the days of three women whose lives have been devoted to working for social change. It tells something about what women organizers think, feel, and do—what happens between the time they leave their houses and come home again, and what happens at home, in their families. This book describes the kinds of work women activists do. There are the door-to-door petition drives and long, tiring speaking tours—in political party work these would be called "whistle stops"—that Florence Luscomb and Ella Baker mention. There is the drudgery of office work, which hovers sometimes in the background of the autobiographies and which sometimes moves to center-stage. There is the answering of telephones, the printing of leaflets, the keeping track of file cards.

Social change work is also making contacts with people in neighborhoods and cities not your own—organization building. Ella Baker describes this in talking about her work organizing in the South for the National Association for the Advancement of Colored People (NAACP). Jessie De La Cruz tells of trips to migrant labor camps, investigating living conditions there, signing up members for the United Farmworkers (UFW).

Since movements that challenge old ideas and that confront people in power are always poor, activists must raise money. Florence Luscomb remembers going to men and women of influence to persuade them that women's suffrage really was a cause worth supporting. Ella Baker recalls traveling through the cities and small towns of the South, drumming up membership for the NAACP.

Constant teaching is an essential part of working for social change. Florence Luscomb goes out on trolley tours of Massachusetts in the first few decades of this century, speaking at factory gates, on street corners, explaining the social conditions of women to crowds of curious onlookers, telling why it is important for women to be able to vote. Ella Baker tells of teaching in the South:

You'd call up Reverend Brother so-and-so, and ask if you could appear before the congregation at such-and-such a time. . . . They'd say, "You have three minutes after the church service." And you'd take it. And you'd use it, to the extent to which you can be persuasive. It's the ammunition you have. That's all you have.

Moving the Mountain tries to show not only how women work in social movements, but why they do this work. Jessie De La Cruz talks of being a farmworker—living in tents surrounded by mud, harvesting acres of rich crops while she and her family often went hungry, seeing children die:

It was claimed if you lifted a young baby up fast, the soft spot would cave in and it would get diarrhea and dehydrate and die. After all these years, I know it wasn't that that killed them. It was hunger, malnutrition, no money to pay the doctors. When the union came, this was one of the things we fought against.

Ella Baker worked in the civil rights movement not only because she heard her grandparents talk about slavery, but because she had grown up seeing her mother help neighbors in
trouble; because she saw her family share food and farm equipment with the rest of the community. A great deal of her vision
of justice and a better world is rooted in the mutual caring of
the black rural community where she grew up. The origins of
Florence Luscomb's political work are partly in her family's
dedication to a wide variety of causes—the antislavery movement of the 1840s, the labor movement of the late nineteenth
century, socialism. Her experience looking for a job in architecture and being told that women would never be hired in that
field also influenced her activism.

If this were a full-length history of women activists in the
United States, it would include many more black, white, His-
panic, Asian American, Native American, and Mexican American women. It would include activists who identify themselves
as lesbians. It would include women of my grandmother's background as well as women who have worked in farm labor and
in factories. The three women in this book—who represent
different movements and who come from different race and
class backgrounds—hint at such variety.

To understand the stories of Ella Baker, Jessie De La Cruz, and
Florence Luscomb, it is important to know something about
the period extending roughly from 1890 to 1920—a time known
as the Progressive Era. That is the period when my grandmother was going to suffrage parades and when Florence
Luscomb was beginning to learn about organizing. It is the
time immediately preceding the stories of Ella Baker and
Jessie De La Cruz. Knowing about those years is to begin
understanding the background of the movements in which the
three women were active. It is also to begin understanding
that the movements in which they worked have not been the
only ones in which women have been active. And it is to begin
knowing more about why movements take the shape they do
among different groups of people.

Suffragists in the Cities

Many of the women in the urban suffrage movement were middle-class white women from the families of business and professional men—women like my grandmother.[2] A blend of economic, legal, and other injustices led these women to the suffrage movement.

During the nineteenth century, women's traditional role in the family was changing. Their mothers and grandmothers had spun and made soap, candles, and other goods in their homes, producing a large part of what their families and communities needed for survival. Most often, the work of male family members was also centered in or around the home. With industrialization, however, much of the work of producing goods was moved out of the home. Most middle-class women continued to work in the home, caring for children, doing housework; it was not considered respectable for these women to hold outside jobs. But with money measuring the worth of one's labor, women's domestic work was no longer considered "valuable." The new wage labor system also meant that middle-class women became financially dependent on their husbands and fathers in a way they had not been when most work was done within the family. For women in the more wealthy families of the middle class, industrialization—especially as it accelerated in the late 1880s—also created an oppressive leisure. These women were at times turned into ornaments, the outward show of the wealth of their fathers and husbands, who were often the owners and managers of the new industries.

Woman's economic dependency was reinforced by her inferior legal status. The early feminist movement that had begun in the 1840s had had some success in improving women's position under the law, especially through the passage of married women's property acts. But, in the period from 1890 to 1920, legal inequities continued to touch every aspect of women's lives: marriage, divorce, education, employment.[3] During this period, women like my grandmother—and women like Florence Luscomb—believed that without political power, little could be done to improve women's condition. To them, the right to vote seemed to be the key that would unlock the door to real influence in many spheres.

Other social movements of the Progressive Era begun by middle-class women were rooted in similar economic, legal, and social circumstances. For example, when Jane Addams launched the settlement house movement and established Hull House in Chicago, she did so in part because of "piteous failures" in her attempts to become "self-dependent." She yearned for an activity in which she could feel socially useful. The movement she initiated was a kind of early social work movement that set up houses offering vocational training, child care, cooking and sewing classes, room and board for women in working-class neighborhoods.[4]

At worst, the middle-class women who worked in movements to aid the working class and poor could be meddling intruders. At best, they gained the respect of the people they met, and they united with them in other efforts. For example, the settlement movement fought battles for child labor laws, for limitations on working hours for women, for industrial health and safety, for the recognition of labor unions.

The Labor Movement

For urban working-class women, industrialization meant long hours of wracking labor in garment factories and textile mills, in dirty, airless lofts and tenement rooms. The conditions under which most women worked were described by one onlooker in 1911:

In a box factory the girls take off their street suits and put on old skirts and waists matted with glue and dirt, in which they spend ten hours a day "scoring," cutting and snipping, wetting great sheets of paper with paste ... lifting the heavy finished boxes back and forth, or deftly covering little ones and throwing them rapidly into a basket, at a few cents a day.

In an overall factory, the light is so poor, and soot-caked windows make it so dim, that some of the women who work there say they cannot stand the eyestrain and will have to work elsewhere.[5]

Because of such conditions, working-class women in this period began trying to organize themselves into unions. But there was also a larger social context in which they struggled. Between 1890 and 1920, a small number of people had gained control over the country's resources. Land, mines, railroads, were dominated by monopolies, the forerunners of today's multinational corporations. While men like Andrew Carnegie and John D. Rockefeller owned the mines, mills, railroads, and factories of the country, the vast majority of people in the United States worked for wages to turn raw materials into useful products. Most of these working people received low wages and lived in poverty. The contrast between their living conditions and those of the rich was dramatic. In 1900, John D. Rockefeller's yearly income was $100 million; a male garment worker in New York earned, on the average, $10 a week—$520 a year if he was employed every week of the year. And women workers earned about half what men did. Such inequalities are expressed forcefully in the best-known union song in the United States, "Solidarity Forever" (to the tune of the "Battle Hymn of the Republic"):

> It is we who plowed the prairies;
>   built the cities where they trade;
> Dug the mines and built the workshops;
>   endless miles of railroad laid.
> Now we stand, outcast and starving,
>   'mid the wonders we have made;
> But the Union makes us strong.[6]

The labor movements of the time came out of reactions to such inequalities of wealth and power. But the labor movement itself was led by men, and generally it aimed at organizing white, male, skilled workers. The American Federation of Labor (AF of L), which dominated the labor movement by the early 1900s, was not interested in organizing unskilled immigrant workers—who by that time were the majority in eastern industries. The AF of L was even less interested in organizing women.[7]

There were a few organizations—mainly socialist ones—that tried to organize the workers the AF of L ignored. For example, the Industrial Workers of the World (IWW) was a revolutionary organization that led some of the major strikes in mining and in the textile industry. Although they sometimes organized women, such organizations were led by men, and when they used the word, "worker," all too often they used it in the sense of *male* worker.

It was in this setting that women workers began their own attempts to organize. Not that they hadn't done so before. From the 1830s on, women spinners and weavers, shoe workers, and women in the needle trades tried to form their own organizations. But it wasn't until the early 1900s that women began organizing in great numbers in the industries of the East and North of the country. In part, this was because there were simply more women in the labor force than before. In part, it was because particular groups of women—Russian Jewish women, for example—brought with them from their countries strong traditions of socialist militancy.

The first large-scale strikes by women during these years were the shirtwaist strikes of New York and Philadelphia in the winter of 1909 to 1910. Other strikes erupted elsewhere— among collar starchers in Troy, New York; among corset makers in Bridgeport, Connecticut. One of the most dramatic strikes of the time was carried forward by twenty-three thousand textile workers in Lawrence, Massachusetts. It was started by women and children, and it was sustained in great part by women. It also brought together a large number of immigrant groups. The Industrial Workers of the World provided the organizers for this strike. One, the young Elizabeth Gurley Flynn, was among the foremost labor organizers of the time. In her autobiography, she describes the special problems of women workers in the Lawrence strike:

There was considerable male opposition to women going to meetings and marching on the picket line. We resolutely set out to combat these notions. The women wanted to picket. We knew that to leave them at home alone, isolated from the strike activity, a prey to worry, affected by the complaints of trades people, landlords, priests and ministers, was dangerous to the strike.[8]

Not many male unionists considered the burdens shouldered by working women—the triple labor of housework, childrearing, and factory labor, for half the wages men earned. One organization, formed by women in 1903, did consider such concerns. The Women's Trade Union League (WTUL) was launched because its founders realized that women needed a special organization if they were ever to become part of the male-dominated trade union movement. The WTUL tried to organize working-class women into existing trade unions and into separate women's unions. Begun by women active in the settlement house movement, as well as by other middle-class women, it gradually drew working-class women into positions of leadership and supported the major women's strikes of the time.

Black Resistance Movements

While white immigrant women were helping fuel the urban labor movement in the first two decades of the century, black women were active in movements of community resistance to racial oppression.[9] The origins of that resistance were in conditions far different from those of either middle- or working-class white women. In slavery, black women had shared a brutal equality in bondage with their men. They were carried as cargo in the holds of the same slave ships; listed on the same bills of sale along with candlesticks, cattle, and silverware; forced to carry the same loads and work the same rows in the fields; lashed and mutilated alongside men. But they were property twice over. They were sold as "breeders," and they suffered as mothers. Moses Grandy, an ex-slave writing after Emancipation, described slave mothers doing field work under the overseer's whip:

Women who had sucking children suffered much from their breasts becoming full of milk [while they were working in the fields], the infants being left at home; they therefore could not keep up with the other hands: I have seen the overseer beat them with raw hide so that the blood and the milk flew mingled from their breasts.[10]

In the community of slaves, black women engaged in sabotage against their masters and mistresses. They aided in revolts. They helped in escapes. They would continue to be leaders in the struggles following Emancipation. Between 1890 and 1920, they led movements against white terrorism, for equal accommodations on railroads, for integration in community and national organizations, for community improvement, for the establishment of black schools and colleges.

The struggle for education was rooted in slavery days, when slave rebellions led to laws forbidding the education of slaves and to tighter enforcement of such laws already in the slave code. Self-education and the education of slaves by some white owners was a subversive act, an act of resistance against mental as well as physical bondage. After Emancipation, a drive for black education began, which has never let up. Black women—for whom teaching has often been considered one of only a few "respectable" jobs—have been particularly active.

Another movement begun by middle-class black women during the period from 1890 to 1920 was the black women's club movement. This originated in black urban communities formed in the North by migrants from the rural South. Within these cities, several generations of educated black women responded to the plight of poor black women and men by forming clubs whose functions were similar to those of the settlement houses. Although led by middle-class women, the black women's clubs also had working-class and poor members. The clubs stressed community betterment, education, and self-improvement. They, of course, differed from similar white movements in putting continual emphasis on race pride and on advancement for all black people.

One of the most courageous movements of the time was closely related to the club movement, drawing much of its support from it. This was a movement of resistance to mass lynchings of black people. In the 1890s, segregation laws were passed, which were to last nearly seventy years. By law, blacks were barred from "white" railroad cars, from "white" eating places and other public facilities. The passing of these laws was accompanied by a wave of terrorism by whites against blacks. In 1895, Ida B. Wells wrote:

Not all or nearly all the murders done by white men, during the past thirty years in the South, have come to light, but the statistics as gathered and preserved by white men, and which have not been questioned, show that during these years more than ten thousand Negroes have been killed in cold blood, without the formality of judicial trial and legal execution. . . . no white man has been lynched for the murder of colored people.[11]

Wells, a journalist whose writing spurred international reaction and black resistance to the massacres, was one of the anti-lynching movement's foremost leaders. So was Mary Church Terrell, a leading club woman and also a suffragist, first president of the National Association of Colored Women (formed in 1896). In 1904, she wrote:

Before 1904 was three months old, thirty-one Negroes had been lynched. Of this number, fifteen were murdered within one week in Arkansas, and one was shot to death in Springfield, Ohio, by a mob composed of men who did not take the trouble to wear masks. Hanging, shooting and burning black men, women and children in the United States have become so common that such occurrences create but little sensation and evoke but slight comment now.[12]

The antilynching movement was instrumental in publicizing the atrocities and, finally, in stemming their tide.[13]

Chicanos and the Struggle for Land

While the roots of black activism are in slavery, the roots of Chicano (Mexican American) activism are in Indian ancestry and a common memory of having been robbed of land that was once theirs. The land robbery began with the invasion of America by Spain in the sixteenth century. The Spaniards burned down villages and murdered the *Indios* (Indians) who resisted their intrusion into the country. What sword and fire didn't finish, disease did: the Spaniards brought smallpox to America, and two-thirds of the *Indios* of Mexico died between the Spanish invasion and 1650.

By the mid-nineteenth century, Mexico included what is now California, New Mexico, Nevada, Utah, Colorado, Wyoming, and part of Arizona. But the United States government changed that. In a war that began in 1846 and that ended in 1848, the United States invaded Mexico, burnt down Mexican villages, and murdered the inhabitants. In the face of such ferocity, Mexico was forced into humiliating surrender. In the town of Guadaloupe Hidalgo, the government signed a treaty that yielded half of what was then Mexico to the United States.

One can't talk about resistance movements among the forebears of a woman like Jessie De La Cruz without talking about Mexico itself in those years. Many Mexicans who would later move to the United States, like Jessie De La Cruz's grandparents, still lived in Mexico and took part in its struggles during the earlier part of the twentieth century.

While Mexico had won independence from Spain in 1821, its own elite controlled the country. The majority of its people were *Indios* and *mestizo* (mixed). They worked in city industries and on *haciendas* (huge estates) owned by a very few large landowners. Under Porfirio Diaz, who ruled the country between 1870 and 1910, Mexico was opened to United States business interests. Billions of North American dollars were invested in Mexican oil, railroads, and mines. In exchange for the "investment," United States businesses received the cooperation of the Mexican rich and the labor of the poor—who, under the arrangement, grew still poorer. Strikes and peasant uprisings spread. For example, in 1906 there was a textile workers' strike near Veracruz, on the west coast of Mexico. It was led by Lucretia Toriz, one of many women active in similar strikes during this time.

In 1910, a revolution began which lasted until 1920. Emiliano Zapata and Pancho Villa, two of the revolution's major leaders, believed firmly that the big *haciendas* should be broken up and the land redistributed to the *Indios*—the peasantry. During the revolution, women were messengers, suppliers of food, and journalists. They also set up army camps, moved munitions and supplies. Some disguised themselves as men and fought in the revolutionary armies.

Diaz was overthrown in 1910. Various men replaced him over the next ten years, but none supported land reform. By the end of the revolution, the government was firmly in the hands of forces friendly to United States business. For the working class and the peasantry, nothing had changed.

Thousands of *Indios* came north to the United States. The men were hired to work in the burgeoning mines, the rapidly expanding railroads, and on the land. The women worked side by side with the men in the fields, harvesting fruits and vegetables in temperatures that soared to 115 degrees. The Chicanos suffered from racism much as blacks did in the South and the East of the country. They were paid lower wages than their Anglo (white) co-workers. They lived in the same kinds of conditions Jessie De La Cruz describes when she talks about her growing up in California. Fieldworkers and miners participated in strikes during this time, but the strikes produced no lasting organizations. The agriculture strikes were crushed by the bloody and violent opposition of the growers. The miners fared little better.

Chicanas (Mexican American women) were active not so much in the early labor efforts of the time—they would become more active in labor strikes in the 1930s—as they were in civil rights and social service work. They worked within mutual aid organizations like the *Alianza Hispano-Americana* (HispanicAmerican Alliance)—groups that offered sickness- and deathbenefits to members. Such groups were early examples of the social service work Jessie De La Cruz describes. Before 1920, Chicanas also worked within the Mexican Liberal party. Founded by Ricardo and Enrique Flores Magon—brothers exiled by Diaz before the revolution—the party called for land reform, equal pay for Chicano workers, an end to United States exploitation of Mexico, and equal rights for women.

Separate and United Struggles

Often, people of the same race or class have worked together in a specific movement for social change. For example, working-class people made up the majority of the labor movement, while middle-class women dominated the suffrage movement. But there have been frequent and important exceptions to this tendency for groups to work in their separate movements. The suffrage movement had strong support from women in the black club movement as well as from rural farm women in the Southwest. In this book, Florence Luscomb tells of organizing laundry workers to support women's suffrage. In the 1930s, Luscomb, a middle-class white woman, worked in the trade union movement. She also joined the National Association for the Advancement of Colored People. She has many counterparts from the mid-nineteenth century through the 1970s. The middle-class women who founded the Women's Trade Union League united with working-class women in their union work. Some—for example, an early WTUL president, Margaret Dreier Robins—also tried to make a bridge between the suffrage movement and women's trade unionism.

Earlier, in the 1840s, Angelina and Sarah Grimké, Elizabeth Cady Stanton, Susan B. Anthony, and others who were to lead the first feminist movement in the United States fought against slavery. The Grimké sisters, daughters of a Charleston slave-owning family, wrote:

The female slaves are our countrywomen—they are our sisters; and to us as women, they have a right to look for sympathy with their sorrows, and effort and prayer for their rescue. . . . Women ought to feel a peculiar sympathy for the colored man's wrong, for like him, she has been accused of mental inferiority, and denied the privileges of a liberal education.[14]

It was in the antislavery movement that women like these learned how to speak publicly; that they wrote their first political articles; that they did their first organizing.

That experience was repeated in the early 1960s, as young, white, middle-class women became active in the civil rights movement. These women participated in drives to register black people to vote, helped set up libraries and classes in small southern towns, and worked in the offices of the movement. They expressed feelings similar to the ones the Grimkés had articulated more than a century before. "The sense of urgency and injustice," wrote one white woman civil rights worker in Mississippi, "is such that I no longer feel I have any choice . . . and every day I feel more and more of a gap between us [in the movement] and the rest of the world that is not engaged in trying to change this cruel system."[15]

There have been splits among different movements, and important mendings of the splits. For example, black, Chicana, Puerto Rican, Asian American, and Native American women were almost entirely absent from the women's liberation movement of the late 1960s and the early 1970s. Sometimes, there was outright hostility, as black women told white women that the feminist movement ignored the issue of racism. But as movements of black people gathered power through the sixties and early seventies, black women formed women's organizations of their own—for example, the National Black Feminist Organization. Also, feminist awareness grew in some radical black organizations, such as the Black Panthers, where women leaders were strong and militant feminists. Finally, there were organizations like the National Welfare Rights Organization that did not define themselves as feminist, but that were feminist in the sense that they developed powerful female leadership and tried to better the condition of large numbers of women.

While Third-World women have begun by feeling that race discrimination is a more important issue than sex discrimination, they have often gone on to fight their special oppression as women within the larger movements of their peoples. These women have experienced the second-class status that women traditionally have had in the family and in institutions outside the family. Indeed, it is within the family that individual, small confrontations often take place—confrontations that lead to a greater political activism by women. For example, Jessie De La Cruz tells of learning how to drive, in secret, after her husband has refused to teach her. She talks about making small but stubborn demands on him in a culture that has expected women to obey their husbands in all things. Much of her story is about how such small steps paved the way for her later militancy and self-consciousness in the United Farmworkers movement.

It is after women of different races have organized their own women's movements that a merging of these movements may take place. The most stunning example of such merging took place at the International Women's Year Conference in Houston, Texas, in November 1977. Black, white, Chicana, Puerto Rican, Asian American, and Native American women joined together in unprecedented solidarity and agreed upon a broad program of social, economic, and political reforms.

Women and Men

One of the special problems that unites all women organizers is the doubt, opposition, and ridicule they almost invariably have faced from the men with whom they have worked. For example, in 1837, as the Grimké sisters began to speak and write in the abolitionist movement, they were denounced in a pastoral letter read from the pulpit and distributed by the General Association of the Congregational Clergy:

The power of woman is in her dependence, flowing from the consciousness of that weakness which God has given her for her protection, and which keeps her in those departments of life that form the character of individuals and of the nation.

But when she assumes the place and tone of a man as a public performer, our care and our protection of her seem unnecessary; we put ourselves in self-defense against her; she yields the power which God has given her for protection, and her character becomes unnatural.[16]

The Grimkés reacted by defending women's capabilities. The men retorted by saying that association with women's rights would damage the antislavery cause. In the summer of 1840, a World Anti-Slavery Convention took place in London. It was attended by an American delegation that included women. After heated debate, the convention ruled that only men could be seated. It was because of that experience and the problems women in the antislavery movement continued to face, that Elizabeth Cady Stanton and others planned the first women's rights convention at Seneca Falls, New York, in 1848.

Again, there are striking similarities between what happened to the founding mothers of feminism and the experiences of some women in the civil rights movement of the 1960s. In 1964, a young black woman, Ruby Doris Smith Robinson, participated in—and possibly led—a sit-in that protested the relegation of women in the student civil rights organization, the Student Nonviolent Coordinating Committee (SNCC), to typing and clerical work. Robinson is said to have written an essay, "The Position of Women in SNCC," and one of the civil rights movement's foremost young male leaders is said to have retorted, "The only position for women in SNCC is prone."[17]

Meantime, women in the northern, largely white student movement of the sixties wrote of a "kind of desperate attempt by men to defend their power by refusing to participate in open public discussion with women."[18] The restiveness women felt in the student movement was also stirring among working women, who resented their exclusion from trade unions still dominated by men. In the early seventies, secretaries and clerical workers—a group whose numbers had skyrocketed since the days of Florence Luscomb's organizing in the 1930s—formed organizations of their own. Boston's 9 to 5, San Francisco's Union WAGE, Chicago's Women Employed, and New York's Women Office Workers were born. These organizations have produced slide shows on the history of secretaries and clerical workers, protested against sexual harassment of women in the workplace, sued employers for back pay and promotion for office workers, and held mock trials of particularly abusive employers. They continue their work through the present.

The difficulties women organizers have encountered echo in Ella Baker's passing reflection on her role in the Southern Christian Leadership Conference (SCLC): "I knew from the beginning that having a woman be an executive of SCLC was not something that would go over with the male-dominated leadership." It echoes, too, in Florence Luscomb's reminiscence that the Congress of Industrial Organizations (CIO) "didn't give much assistance in having secretaries organized. They'd be too busy trying to organize the . . . large important bodies of the working class." They echo, finally, in Jessie De La Cruz's memory of her early organizing days. "It was very hard being a woman organizer. Some of our people my age and older were raised with the old customs in Mexico: where the husband rules, he is king of his house. . . . So when we first started it was very, very hard. Men gave us the most trouble. . . . They were for the union, but they were not taking orders from women, they said."

Male opposition to female activism is rooted in the traditional superior status of men in and outside of families, and in men's reluctance to give up that superiority. Jessie De La Cruz's remark reminds us that in organizing, women have been forced to think about their "place" at home. They have been forced to think about this both because men have insisted on reminding them of it, and because marriage and parenthood—especially parenthood—have placed greater demands on women than on men. In the mid-nineteenth century, Elizabeth Cady Stanton raised seven children while she lectured and produced reams of writing. To her dearest friend and political comrade, Susan B. Anthony, she wrote letters that mixed political and household talk:

Can you get any acute lawyer . . . to look up just eight laws concerning us—the very worst in all the code? I can generalize and philosophize easily enough of myself; but the details of the particular laws I need, I have not time to look up. You see, while I am about the house, surrounded by my children, washing dishes, baking, sewing, etc., I can think up many points, but I cannot search books, for my hands as well as my brains would be necessary for that work. . . . I seldom have one hour undisturbed in which to sit down and write. Men who can, when they wish to write a document, shut themselves up for days with their thoughts and their books, know little of what difficulties a woman must surmount to get off a tolerable production.[19]

Men working in political movements have rarely thought twice about marriage and parenthood. Women have had to think a good deal more. In balancing the demands of political work and life at home, they have often leaned on each other. The remarkable fifty-year-long friendship between Stanton and Anthony is one of the most famous examples of relationships that have been very usual among women activists. The two women worked together in a way that made the most of the special skills of each. Stanton was a keen organizer of ideas; Anthony was a skillful handler of large campaigns and meetings, and a powerful speaker. They merged their talents, Stanton often writing the talks that Anthony went on to deliver.[20]

In the life of Florence Luscomb, who never married, the deep friendship with her mother laid the foundations for her later work, and gave her continuing support. Her friendships with other women activists have enriched her life. Among younger women, the tradition of female friendship and mutual support in political work has continued. Perhaps women haven't written about these relationships because they have taken them for granted. But the friendships have been very fruitful.

For example, *Our Bodies, Ourselves,* an extremely popular, comprehensive book on women's physiology, sexuality, and health, was written in 1971 by a group of Boston women whose personal and political friendships have lasted through the present.[21]

While women activists in the sixties relied on each other for support, they also began demanding that men in their organizations take on the burdens of what earlier had been considered "women's work": brewing coffee, washing dishes, cleaning offices. Someone must do the typing and clerical work, and the large job of child care. Generally, male organizers have left it up to women in the organizations to do such work. But with the growth of the women's movement, a new awareness spread among women that they could change the habits of the past. For example, under women's pressure, many organizations in the late sixties and early seventies passed rules stating that at meetings, rooms had to be set aside for child care, supplied with toys, and staffed by men in the organizations. The demand for shared child care came out of a recognition that just because women bear children, they need not have full responsibility for rearing them. "Women," stated a National Organization for Women press release in December 1970, "will never have full opportunities to participate in our economic, political, cultural life as long as they bear this responsibility almost entirely alone and isolated from the larger world. . . . We reject the idea that mothers have a special child care role that is not to be shared equally by the fathers."

In many organizations, people tried to share all kinds of work. Those who made public speeches were asked to clean the office and do other routine tasks. Those who usually volunteered for routine work were encouraged to learn how to chair meetings and speak publicly. The ideal of sharing work was valued especially among feminists, since women were particularly sensitive to having been excluded from equal participation in the past.

While such ideals didn't always work in practice, they were part of an important vision that replaced traditional notions of the way power is exerted. Usually organizations—schools, factories, offices—are run from the top down. A group of people make decisions and give orders to managers who pass the orders to the people at the bottom. The activists of the sixties imagined a new society in which authority would be shared, in which cooperation would replace competition, in which differences in wealth and power would be abolished, in which a real democracy would come into being.

Moving the Mountain

The title of this book, *Moving the Mountain*, is taken from a utopian novel written by Charlotte Perkins Gilman in 1911. Gilman, a feminist author, activist, and lecturer, described in her book a future that seemed impossible—a future in which sexual differences would not stop people from choosing the work they wanted to do, in which all work was enjoyable, in which poverty and racism no longer existed. Many of the evils Gilman "abolished" in her book still exist today; they make up a world that often seems as hard to change as it might be to move mountains. Yet activists have tried and succeeded, and will continue to do so.

In the stories that follow, Florence Luscomb, Ella Baker, and Jessie De La Cruz tell about their own struggles to move the mountain in their lifetimes. All three women share a particular style of leadership. They have been influential wherever they have worked, revered by those who have worked with them and by the people among whom they have organized. But they aren't superstars, nor have they tried to be. They have been behind-the-scenes leaders who have worked to build strength, self-confidence, skills, and commitment in others. All three believe that while organizers and leaders may inspire people, help them think through problems and shape goals, it is finally the people themselves, at the grassroots, who must bring about a future that is still only in our imaginings.

ELLEN CANTAROW

Moving
the Mountain

Women Working for Social Change

ONE:
Florence Luscomb

For Suffrage, Labor, and Peace

By Sharon Hartman Strom

WOMEN VOTE

WE DEMAND AN AMENDMENT TO THE CONSTITUTION OF THE UNITED STATES ENFRANCHISING THE WOMEN OF THIS COUNTRY

On International Women's Day in 1970, several hundred women gathered in Boston to hear Florence Luscomb speak. Although many knew about her legendary activism of over sixty years, some had never seen Luscomb before. As she mounted a low platform and began to speak, the women who had come to celebrate the day realized just how old Luscomb was—eighty-three, to be exact. Her age seemed an embodiment of history, a history women were just beginning to rediscover in the late 1960s. Luscomb talked that day about the struggle for women's rights in the nineteenth century, about a time when women "didn't even own their own clothes if they were married." And she spoke at length about her life of activism, a life

CHRONOLOGY

1887: Florence Luscomb born, Lowell, Massachusetts.

1888: Parents separate and Florence moves to Boston with her mother, Hannah Luscomb.

1909: Graduates from M.I.T. and begins work as an architect.

1911–18: Visits London and Stockholm to observe the international suffrage movement. Joins the National Association for the Advancement of Colored People. Leaves architecture work to become a full-time suffrage organizer.

1920–22: Executive secretary of Mass. League of Women Voters. Runs for Boston City Council and is narrowly defeated.

1922–28: Does prison reform work for Mass. Civic League. Campaigns for Progressive party presidential candidate, LaFollette. Factory inspector for Joint Board of Sanitary Control (ILGWU).

1929–33: Executive secretary of Mass. Women's International League for Peace and Freedom; recruits Afro-American women for the League's Board.

1934–36: Tours British Isles and Soviet Union. Works in labor movement. Runs for Congress on People's Labor party ticket.

1937–47: Organizes clerical workers. Attends founding convention of the United Office and Professional Workers of America (CIO) and becomes first president of the Boston local. Works in antifascist and Spanish relief movements and with the American Civil Liberties Union. Builds cabin in New Hampshire.

1948–50: Directs Henry Wallace for President campaign in Maine. Runs for Congress, then for governor of Massachusetts, on the Progressive party ticket. Vice-president of Boston NAACP.

1953–55: Blacklisted and redbaited. Writes first anti-Vietnam war leaflet distributed in Boston.

1956–59: Fights anti-Communist legislation and raises money for victims of redbaiting.

1960–62: Visits Cuba and China. Attends Tokyo Conference on A- and H-bombs.

1963–present: Active in civil rights, antiwar, and women's movements.

in which a passion for justice for women overflowed and became a passion for human rights in general.

Her earliest political work was in the woman suffrage campaign in the first two decades of the century. During the 1920s, she worked in the National Association for the Advancement of Colored People (NAACP) and joined the newly-formed American Civil Liberties Union (ACLU). Around the same time, she began her long involvement in the labor movement, inspecting health and safety conditions in garment factories for the International Ladies Garment Workers' Union. In the early thirties, she was executive secretary for the Massachusetts branch of the Women's International League for Peace and Freedom (WILPF), a peace organization formed in World War I. Later in the thirties, she was a pathbreaker in organizing women office workers, and she became the first president of the Boston local of the United Office and Professional Workers of America (UOPWA). The UOPWA was a union within the new, struggling Congress of Industrial Organizations (CIO), which arose in the 1930s to challenge the conservative American Federation of Labor (AF of L) and to organize the unskilled, immigrant, and black workers the AF of L had traditionally ignored.

In 1952, Luscomb ran for governor of Massachusetts on the ticket of the Progressive party—a third party that opposed the anti-Communist policies of the Truman administration. She worked in the peace movement and continued in the struggle to end racial discrimination in the fifties. By the sixties, a larger and more vigorous left welcomed her as a participant in the antiwar and civil rights movements.

Florence Luscomb is slightly bent, white-haired, thin—a woman with a disarming smile and an unfailingly friendly greeting. Her animated face is lined with wrinkles, and as she tells anecdotes, her brown eyes twinkle and her hands move in emphatic gestures. She lives in a cooperative house with a group of men and women at least fifty years younger than she. She divides her year between the house in Boston in the winter and her cabin in New Hampshire during the summer. Since 1939, she has spent every summer except two in a small one-room log house in a clearing in the woods at the base of Mount Chocorua, surrounded by her vegetable garden, trees, and flowers. She has no electricity, no running water, and no indoor plumbing. She chops wood for her small cook stove, buries the refuse from her chemical toilet, plants her own garden, and eats her own vegetables.

Her political activism has been a way of life. When she was young, her mother, Hannah Knox Luscomb, took her to suffrage meetings and socialist rallies and imbued her with a sense of responsibility for the plight of people far different from her own, upper-middle-class family. Hannah Luscomb was an independent woman who balanced political activism with pleasure, physical exercise, and work. Her daughter carried that example of balanced living into her adulthood. When Florence Luscomb joined a group or worked against social injustice, she often did those things with friends who shared her political ideas. Not only was there the making up of leaflets, the long speaking tours, the quest for funds for struggling young organizations, but there were also hikes in the White Mountains and festive suppers with lingering, laughing conversations. Luscomb has had friends as close to her as sisters—all of whom she met in the course of her activism. For instance, Zara duPont, an older woman Luscomb first met in the suffrage movement, lived near Luscomb in Cambridge, Massachusetts, in the thirties, and the two women walked on strikers' picket lines together.* In 1939, they wore gas masks on a picket line in Everett, Massachusetts, to protest police brutality. But they also took a train trip across the country to see the United States with a friend from Europe. Luscomb's best friend, Mary Duggan, was long a co-worker in the American Civil Liberties Union. Duggan has a cabin next door to Luscomb, and the two women have toured Scotland together, shared jokes, and helped each other through hard times.

Successful male reformers and radicals often parlay their triumphs into national office, but Luscomb has preferred to stay in Boston, deepening ties with her local community and

---

* Zara duPont came from the Kentucky branch of the fabulously wealthy duPont family. The duPonts settled in Delaware in the eighteenth century and became major producers of chemicals and munitions. By the early twentieth century, they were among the most powerful industrialists in the world. Zara duPont refused to be a debutante and have a "coming out" party; she later became a suffragist and peace activist, and used her position as a major stockholder in several corporations to protest against unfair labor practices.

friends, rather than moving on to wider spheres. Not that she has never been outside of Boston. In the campaign for woman suffrage, she traveled to the Midwest and the South. In 1911, she visited England and the Continent to study the British and international suffrage movements; she took a job in 1934 as a chauffeur for an elderly woman and drove through the British Isles. She vacationed in the Soviet Union in 1935, was in Cuba in 1961 when the United States broke relations with Fidel Castro, and went to China in 1962. She also has climbed Mount Washington five times, kissed the Blarney Stone, and ridden a mule to the bottom of the Grand Canyon.

Luscomb once advised a good friend that "there is no end to what you can accomplish if you don't care who gets the credit." She has never pushed to be a leader. On the contrary, she has consistently taken jobs that require hard work, rather than ones leading to self-importance or fame. While the first period of Luscomb's life was spent in the women's movement, which steadily declined in the 1920s, Luscomb went on to work in activist groups dominated by men, groups often as sexist as the surrounding society. The contributions of women often went unrecognized. It did not occur to the members of the American Civil Liberties Union or the Massachusetts CIO that women might have headed their groups. The chief exception to this general rule is the Boston NAACP, which in 1947 made Luscomb and Lucille LeSeuer, a close friend from the black community, vice-president and president of the Boston chapter.

Luscomb's history as a social activist was recovered by the women's movement of the late sixties. Boston feminists, anxious to learn about the struggles their great-grandmothers had waged for equal rights, began to invite Luscomb to meetings and classes. Since then, she has traveled all over the Northeast and as far west as St. Louis to speak about the history of the women's movement.

On February 6, 1977, friends of Luscomb gathered at the Community Church of Boston to hear her speak, to present her with the second annual Sacco and Vanzetti award, and to celebrate her ninetieth birthday. Given in memory of Niccolo Sacco and Bartolomeo Vanzetti, two Italian immigrant anarchists who dedicated their lives to fighting for working people, the award was instituted by the Community Church in 1975 to honor "a living fighter." In her talk, Luscomb carried her audience back to her mother's activism, then to the suffrage work of her own youth. She made radical unionism live again for those who had only read about it. She bore her audience along with her in the fights to prevent the development of nuclear weapons, to end segregation. And many who were listening remembered her continuous work in the movement against the Vietnam war.

When she was done, representatives from a score of Boston activist groups stepped forward to tell how Luscomb had influenced their lives and the work of their organizations. Time and again they invoked the same themes: Luscomb worked more than she talked. She had the courage of her convictions. She never abandoned political causes because they were unpopular. She had taught many a fledgling activist how to write a leaflet, give a speech, or lobby the state house. The last speaker was a young woman from 9 to 5, a group that has been organizing clerical workers in Boston. "We, your granddaughters," she said, "will have the example of your life to give us inspiration and confidence."

Growing Up

It was the boast of the founders of the republic, that the rights for which they contended were the rights of human nature. Woman has not been a heedless spectator of the events of this century, nor a dull listener to the grand arguments for the equal rights of humanity. From the earliest history of our country woman has shown equal devotion with man to the cause of freedom, and has stood firmly by his side in its defense. Together, they have cemented the stones of every monument man has reared to liberty.

And now, at the close of a hundred years, as the hour-hand of the great clock that marks the centuries points to 1876, we declare our faith in the principles of self-government; our full equality with man in natural rights; that woman was made first for her own happiness, with the absolute right to herself—to all the opportunities and advantages life affords for her complete development; and we deny that dogma of the centuries, incorporated in the codes of all

nations—that woman was made for man—her best interests in
all cases, to be sacrificed to his will. We ask of our rulers, at this hour,
no special favors, no special privileges, no special legislation. We
ask justice, we ask equality, we ask that all the civil and political
rights that belong to citizens of the United States, be guaranteed to
us and our daughters forever.

—Declaration of Rights for Women by the National Woman
Suffrage Association, read by Susan B. Anthony in front of
Independence Hall, July 4, 1876.

Florence Luscomb believes that her mother made her a radical.
Hannah Knox Luscomb was the daughter of a prosperous lawyer who joined an antislavery political party—the Republican
party—in the slave state of Missouri in the Civil War era. As a
child, Florence Luscomb heard how her grandfather had paced
the floor all night after learning of the death of the fiery abolitionist John Brown.*

During her twenties, Hannah Knox became her father's
housekeeper and then married an artist. In the 1880s, women
rarely were able to divorce their husbands, and society frowned
on wives who refused to stay in unhappy marriages. Hannah
Knox Luscomb took the unusual step of leaving her husband in
1888 and setting up a separate household with her infant daughter Florence. She was able to do this because she had inherited a
substantial estate from her maternal grandmother. Most
women of the nineteenth century would not have been so economically independent, and thirty years earlier, Hannah Luscomb's husband would have had legal rights to all his wife's
property and income.

The married women's property acts of the 1860s and 1870s,
which made it possible for women to own the property they
brought into marriage, were among the first accomplishments
of the nineteenth-century women's movement, a movement

---

* The abolitionists were the most radical element of the antislavery movement
between 1830 and 1865. They argued that Afro-American slaves should be freed
immediately and that their owners should not receive any monetary compensa-
tion. John Brown led a small band of white abolitionists and black freedmen on
the federal arsenal at Harper's Ferry, Virginia, in 1859, hoping to seize the arms
there and spark a slave insurrection throughout the South. The raid failed, and
Brown was executed by the state of Virginia.

Hannah Luscomb first heard described by Wendell Phillips. Phillips was one of the most courageous and outspoken of all the Boston abolitionists. He saw logical connections between the struggles for black civil rights, women's rights, and trade unions for working people. Hannah Luscomb believed she had a mission to carry the political idealism of her father forward another generation, and she adopted the causes advocated by Phillips and other New England radicals. She joined the Massachusetts woman suffrage movement, and she also became a member of the Knights of Labor, one of the first national labor organizations in the United States. In the 1890s, she joined the Populist party, which fought for economic justice for farmers and an end to monopolistic railroads. She protested American and European invasions of Third World countries through membership in the Anti-Imperialist League. She became a disciple of Edward Bellamy, a Massachusetts social reformer who believed that socialism could provide a utopian world in which class and ethnic differences would disappear. She also joined the Socialist party.[1]

Florence Luscomb grew up in a serene and comfortable nineteenth-century home. That home was a curious combination of middle-class propriety and social activism. Hannah Luscomb adored her beautiful daughter; she dressed her in lovely clothes and saw that she was well-educated in traditional schools. At the same time, she introduced her to all the political causes she believed in. As Florence became older, her mother stepped back to let her play a more prominent role in various social movements. Hannah and Florence Luscomb lived together until Hannah's death in 1933. During that long time, Florence Luscomb had her mother to come home to, a mother who continued to provide loving support for all the things she was doing. Florence Luscomb is now in her nineties; tears still come to her eyes when she speaks of her mother. No other person in her life was ever as important to her.

My mother's ancestors came over here before the revolution, settled out in the Berkshires in Massachusetts. They were mainly farmers, and they fought in the Revolution. My grandfather graduated from Williams College and Harvard Law School, and

became a lawyer. He was a member of Congress during the Civil War. Mother was born in 1848, and her mother died when she was eleven or twelve years old. Two of her brothers were lawyers, and her uncle was Chief Justice of the Supreme Court of Massachusetts. It was a legal family.

Mother had a great contempt for the law. She'd heard all these lawyers getting together all their friends, telling about how they won this case—got some crook who was guilty off on a technicality, you know. So she didn't think of the law as being justice. Her father was in the Republican party at the time of the Civil War, and that was the progressive political movement of the times. As a young woman, she heard Wendell Phillips speak on women's rights. He didn't convert her. She simply said, "Why, of course those are the things I believe."

The thing that makes me feel that she is so significant is that she associated herself with labor, and with working people, and with socialism, which was not for her own personal needs, but just from a sense of brotherhood, and justice, and righteousness. She had the moral attitude. Mother thought her way through all of these labor and radical movements. She wasn't brought up by her family in them, but she worked out her own philosophy. And that's a really independent spirit. As a young woman, mother left the orthodox Protestant church. She said that all of the regular churches supported the status quo. She was a very religious woman all her life. She read the Bible, she believed in Christianity and its doctrines. But the regular churches, she said, do not support the needs of the common people. They are the supporters of the status quo. In a time when woman's place was in the home, she allied herself with progressive thought. Before the American Federation of Labor was formed, the first labor movement was the Knights of Labor. My mother, a woman, joined it. She joined the old Populist party, a radical political party of the time. She was in the women's movement.

Mother was thirty-one years old when she married, and the marriage broke up when I was a year and a half old. Mother took me to Boston then. My father of course was nothing in my life; he used to see us once or twice a year. We lived in apartments chiefly. We had a housekeeper; she did all the cooking and of course kept the house clean. And one time the neighbors came in with a very indignant delegation because my mother was paying her housekeeper more than the customary amount, and their maids were all complaining.

I was just young, and mother was going to all sorts of meetings—social meetings, suffrage meetings—about all sorts of public issues. She took me, for example, to hear Eugene V. Debs speak.* He was campaigning for the presidency. It was a rally down in Lynn. We had to get up at six in the morning to get down there in time to hear him at an open-air rally. She was a delegate to the National American Woman Suffrage Association Convention in 1892, and she took me with her, as a five-year-old child. Then I heard Susan B. Anthony speak. I'm probably the only living American who has heard Susan B. Anthony speak. Mother never tried to dictate what I should believe in. But I went to meetings with her, she exposed me to the thoughts, she had leaflets, she had reading matter around for me to read if I wanted to. We were interested in Dickens. And she did a great deal of reading aloud to me. We read practically all Dickens aloud.

When I was old enough to go to school you couldn't go to school without being vaccinated. Mother took me to a doctor to get me vaccinated, and this doctor had had a son die from an improper vaccination. He berated mother and told her the dangers of it all, so he converted her to believe that she shouldn't have me vaccinated. So she had to send me to private schools. And the private school, which was at that time both a grammar school and a high school, was Chauncy Hall. The high school was especially a preparatory school for MIT [Massachusetts Institute of Technology], and that's how I got the idea of going to MIT. All of my boy classmates were going to MIT—why shouldn't I go?

When I went to MIT I had about a six-mile walk every day, and then one of the boys and I used to go off every Sunday on long walks. I've walked anywhere up to twenty miles on a Sunday.

* Eugene V. Debs was a life-long fighter for social justice and industrial unionism. He began as a labor organizer for the railroad workers in the 1890s and then helped organize the Socialist party. He was universally described by those who heard him speak as one of the greatest orators of all time.

When I was a child, mother would take me out on picnics; we'd go out in the country. One of my *earliest* recollections—I don't suppose I was more than three years old—was running up to my mother in ecstasy with a dandelion that I'd found. I just loved flowers. I expected to be a landscape architect, and Tech had the course in landscape architecture. But it had been dwindling, and the year I entered I was the only one who applied, so that they dropped it that year.

I graduated from MIT as an architect in '09. And women in architecture were very, very few, and among the architects there was great discrimination against hiring any women as draftsmen. It was rather the custom for the boys in the class, in order to get practical experience to supplement the theoretical knowledge they were getting in college, to go out after their sophomore year and take a job in an architect's office, and work all summer without any pay. And I thought, well, if it was important for the boys to get this experience, I would get it. But I knew that a great many architects would not hire any women. I went to eleven of them before I found one that would take me in, even to work for nothing for them. One man told me, "Why, I sent to Tech and said I would like one of their architectural students to work this summer, but, I never thought of having a woman." And he wouldn't take me in. And finally, one man took me on, and after the second week he came around, and said, "Well, I think it's only fair that I pay you enough to cover your carfare and your lunches." And he laid down two dollars on my desk.

I learned in school that the American government was founded on the principle that all men are created equal. But there was no equality for half the human race—my half. Women were discriminated against not only in political freedom, but in their professional and work opportunities, in their pay, in many of their laws and social conditions and customs. And I burned with indignation at this injustice. So all through school days, I did what a youngster could do. I ushered at meetings, and handed out leaflets, and addressed envelopes. And after I graduated from MIT in '09, I then took an active part in the fight for women's rights and women's votes.

The Suffrage Movement

*What a big thing Votes for Women really is. . . . If it just meant
votes it would hardly be worth working for, neither would it require
much work, for . . . progressive men . . . would accept it as readily
as other progressive ideas. But they . . . [don't] accept it, so it must be
that it stands for a more significant change than just the casting
of votes. . . . Ought women to have less self-respect than men!
I think that's the point of the whole matter. . . . It is in that that the
symbolism and the chief value of the ballot lies. And when
womanhood wakes to the fact that it also is human . . . then there
will be changes.*

—Letter from Florence Luscomb to a friend, 1914.

The organized women's movement of the nineteenth century
made its first appearance in 1848, the year Hannah Knox Luscomb was born. A group of women who had been active in the
antislavery and temperance* movements gathered together to
ratify a Declaration of Sentiments in the tiny village of Seneca
Falls, New York. The Declaration shaped the goals of the
women's movement for the rest of the century. It listed the demands of women who wanted their rights: the right to control
inherited property, to divorce, to retain custody over children,
to equal pay, to equal education, and to fundamental equality
under the law. Surprisingly, the demand that drew the most
hostility from men was the one for the right to vote.

By the time Hannah Luscomb joined the women's movement in Boston in the 1880s, the original wide-sweeping goals
of feminists had narrowed. Having made progress in such matters as education and property rights, the movement settled on
suffrage as its major goal. Although many feminists had not forgotten such issues as better working conditions for working
women or equal pay for equal work, bitter experience had

---

* Feminists in the nineteenth century often joined the temperance movement
since they felt that excessive drinking was a woman's issue. Unable to find jobs
that paid enough to support their families, and without the right to divorce,
women with alcoholic husbands were often condemned to lives of abuse and
misery. Elizabeth Cady Stanton and Susan B. Anthony, two of the most radical
feminists of the nineteenth century, held national offices in the Daughters of
Temperance in the 1850s before going on to more clear-cut feminist activity.

proven that without political power, little could be done about them. More and more it seemed as though the vote had to come first.

In the 1860s, the suffrage movement had split into two groups. One faction, based in Washington, D.C., worked for the suffrage on a national basis, advocating a federal amendment to the United States Constitution. A larger group, based in Massachusetts, worked for the suffrage on a state by state basis, hoping to get women the right to vote on the local level. By the 1890s, when the two groups merged to form the National American Woman Suffrage Association (NAWSA), little progress had been made with either strategy. Only a few of the far western states, with small populations of women, had granted woman suffrage. In a few eastern communities, women could vote for members of their school committees. The federal amendment had yet to reach the floor of the Congress.

By the time Florence Luscomb joined the woman suffrage movement in the early twentieth century, conditions were rapidly changing. Luscomb was typical of a new generation of self-confident and well-educated young women who were willing to carry their demand for the vote to the streets. They were spurred on by a vigorous international woman suffrage movement and were especially inspired by the militant activism of the British suffragettes. Luscomb went to London in 1911 and studied the British movement for several weeks. There she saw many of the tactics American suffragists borrowed from their British sisters. Women spoke in open-air meetings on the street to whomever would listen; they marched in huge parades; they worked to defeat political candidates opposed to women's suffrage. American suffragists also began to lobby state legislatures and bombard officeholders with petitions from constituents. They began to convert many politicians to woman suffrage.

The national suffrage association and state suffrage groups now worked in close cooperation. A corps of women worked in Washington, D.C., to get the federal amendment through Congress, and hundreds of determined women crisscrossed the country to win the suffrage in individual states. A small minority even picketed the White House and were arrested. Women had the vote by 1920.

The vote seemed to attract large numbers of women to feminism in a way that no other cause could; by 1917, two million women belonged to the National American Woman Suffrage Association. Of course, suffrage was among the least controversial of women's issues, one around which women of many different political persuasions and classes could rally. From Socialists to Republicans, from Afro-American club women to white Protestant aristocrats, many women could agree that the vote was an important step toward real equality.

The fight for woman suffrage also took place during a period of enormous political optimism, when many different groups of people believed that changing the law could fundamentally change the way people behaved. In this "Progressive Era," running from about 1895 to 1920, many Americans sought relief from political and economic problems through legislation. Women quite naturally turned to the amendment process to gain a measure of liberation.

Women felt that after winning the vote they could use it for the good of society. They said that they would especially be concerned with the plight of working women and the shocking conditions of child labor. They said they would work for peace and clean up the cities of America. They promised to end political corruption in Washington. They made, in other words, a lot of promises they would not be able to keep.

Whatever the outcome of suffrage for women, Florence Luscomb gained an invaluable personal and political education during her years of work for the vote. She learned to speak before any kind and size of audience, under any conditions. She learned how to drive a car and repair it, an experience few women were likely to have at that time. She met men and women from every walk of life. She learned to handle hostile audiences, arrogant club women, imperious state legislators, devout churchgoers. She made scores of friends. The camaraderie which these women shared, as they toured the countryside or leafleted the cities, left them with a network of personal friendships which lasted for years. As Luscomb wrote to a friend in 1914, the need to obtain the right to vote was largely psychological, for it was in many ways the last taunting symbol of her inequality. She had proven to herself that she could do almost everything else.

I graduated from college in '09, and then I took a job as an architectural draftsman, but all my spare time I put in on the suffrage movement. I was working with one of the women who had graduated with a very brilliant record from MIT, Ida Annah Ryan. She lived in Waltham, so she set up her architectural office there, and I went out and was a draftsman for her. Well, she was very deeply interested in suffrage, just as I was, so she was always willing to let me off when there was any particular job to be done. In 1915, when we had the suffrage referendum here, I took all the summertime and worked on that. Then the First World War came along, and in the time of world war, there is no architectural work. There's no labor available for building, there's no material available, and they won't even give you building permits. So we had no work at all. I put in all my spare time as a volunteer in the suffrage association, so then when my regular job folded, I took a paid position. I was the assistant executive secretary for the Boston Equal Suffrage Association.

The year I graduated from college, four women started to try out street meetings in small towns. Soon they were running a regular schedule of meetings every Saturday, and I made my speaking debut on a soapbox in Dedham. By midsummer, the secretary of the Massachusetts Woman Suffrage Association planned a trolley-tour of Massachusetts. This was before autos were commonplace. We toured the state, speaking at factory gates, crossroads, and in the hearts of cities. For years, street meetings were held in every section of Boston every summer.

We did every possible publicity stunt to keep suffrage in the public mind. When the circus came to Waltham, where I was working as an architectural draftsman, we interviewed the owner of the traveling circus when they arrived at 5:00 A.M. We got him to hang a large painted banner, "Votes for Women," on the elephant in the parade. We had a float in the Fourth of July parade. We took over the local Waltham newspaper for one day,

(text continued on page 20)

LEGENDARY ACTIVIST

Far right: Florence Luscomb, campaigning for suffrage. **1**: Luscomb, center, selling *The Woman's Journal* on a street corner. **2**: Luscomb speaking at a women office workers' rally, Boston, 1974. **3**: Luscomb as a young woman, with her friends. **4**: Progressive party campaign poster, Luscomb for Governor, 1952. **5**: Luscomb with U.N. Vietnamese delegation. **6**: At her New Hampshire cabin. **7**: Participating in an antiwar demonstration, 1971. **8**: Florence Luscomb picnicking with her mother, Hannah Luscomb.

the
PEACE
candidate
for
Governor

LORENCE H. LUSCOMB

FLORENCE LUSCOMB

8

19

wrote all the news and edited the paper and had feature articles, such as on women taxpayers in the city, on business and professional women, and so forth. Of course, all this stir of publicity and activity meant a vast increase in indoor meetings also, big and little. I did much speaking before audiences of every kind and size, indoors and out.

In 1912, Ohio was having a state referendum and mother and I went there to work, most of the time in Youngstown. In 1914, I worked in Ohio's second referendum, this time in the traveling troupe, under Zara duPont, covering the rural areas.

I was working by myself then, through a certain district. They were trying to find some people in each community who might form a little group that would arrange for the later meetings. I called on all of the important people and heads of the churches. And I talked to the minister, and he was very strongly in favor of women's suffrage. He said, "It's too bad you're not here on a Sunday, because I would let you speak in my church." Well, a few weeks later I was in a nearby town, on a Saturday, and I didn't have any engagement on a Sunday. So I wrote to him, and he arranged to have me be there on Sunday. So on Sunday morning, I presented myself at the door of the church. He greeted me and then he said, "You know, my congregation would expect to hear from me somewhat today, so what I've planned is that I will talk for twenty minutes and then I will introduce you and you can talk for twenty minutes." So I sat up on the platform with him while he conducted the service, and then he preached for twenty minutes. And he preached on Moses and Aaron going down before Pharoah. Aaron threw down his rod, and turned it into a serpent, and he said this was a message from God. The minister said, "Was it a beautiful golden staff? No, it was just an ordinary stick that Aaron had picked up along the roadside to help him trudge along." He said, "God can use anything as a messenger. Even a crooked stick. We have one of these messengers from God here with us today." And then he introduced *me*.

Meanwhile, Massachusetts suffragists had gone into politics, working against members of the legislature who were outstanding opponents of the vote for women. The man who was speaker of the house in our legislature here had indulged in all sorts of political schemes to defeat the suffrage amendment.

When we filed the bill to amend the state constitution, he would refer it to a committee that was stacked in opposition to it. And then, when they reported it out, he would call it up for a vote at some time when there was a small audience. He just used every possible trick as the Speaker of the House to defeat any suffrage law. So we went out and campaigned against him, and we defeated him.

In 1915, we had a referendum in Massachusetts for an amendment to the state constitution.[2] By that time, we had organizations in all the big cities and the important towns. But in the small towns we didn't have any contacts. So we got two little automobiles of four workers in each one, and between them, they covered the state spending a day in each community. We'd go there in the morning, and we'd canvass the whole town with leaflets, talking to any of the men that we could catch. If there was a farmer in the field, we'd run out and talk to him, or if he wasn't home, we'd talk to his wife, and leave leaflets for him. We had all these leaflets: "Why the mother needs to vote so she can control the conditions of the education and health that affect her children." "Why the working woman needs to vote so that she can have something to say about the laws." "Why the tax-paying woman ought to vote, so she can say how her money should be spent." So we would canvass that day. If there was a little local industry in town, perhaps a little sawmill or something, we'd go there at noon and hand out leaflets. Some would come back at half-past twelve for a meeting, and then we would stand up and speak until the whistle blew at one. And then, that evening, we would have an open-air rally in the heart of the town in front of the post office or the general store. Or, if there was an East Podunck and a West Podunck, we'd have one meeting at seven and the other at eight. I was in charge of one of those little automobile parties. I did all of the speaking, and that's when I made two hundred and twenty-two speeches in fourteen weeks. I haven't been afraid to face an audience since!

We had a young man who was hired as the chauffeur for our party. Here I was spending all these weeks driving around over the backroads of the state, so when we were going from one town to another, he showed me how to drive. I learned to drive over the worst roads, and the result was I had perfect control of the car. And at that time the only thing you had to do was to send in a sworn statement that you had driven one hundred miles. So I drove more than one hundred miles, and I sent it in, and I got my driving license.

Two of the most effective bits of propaganda of the referendum campaign were the two great parades held in Boston in 1914 and '15. We made a great effort to have a contingent in the parade of working women. My own special job was to get women laundry workers as one section in that parade. At that time, we didn't have any automatic laundry machines. If you didn't go down and scrub out your own clothes, and set tubs in the cellar, you could take them to local laundries where they would be done. And so I visited practically all the women's laundries in Boston at noontime, and spoke to the women, and urged them to come out and march in this suffrage parade. We had a little section of women laundry workers. And other people had done the same with other women in industry, so that we had a working woman's section in our parade. Just why seeing women walk down the street in parade should convince men to vote for suffrage is a mystery, but it did so by the thousands. Probably because it gave them visual proof that the women who wanted the suffrage were ordinary representative women—homemakers, mothers, daughters, teachers, working women—and not the unsexed freaks the antis declared they were.

After the federal amendment was passed, then it was coming up to the various states to be ratified. In Massachusetts, it was referred to a committee of the legislature to bring in a recommendation as to how they should or should not ratify it. And the suffrage association felt that recommendation would be entirely determined by the attitude of the chairman of the committee. He lived somewhere up in northeastern Massachusetts, and they weren't sure what his attitude would be—he'd never committed himself. So just about a week before the committee was going to bring in its recommendation, the state organization decided they ought to do more to bring pressure on this chairman, whose name I have forgotten, because it was a long time ago.

They sent me up in charge of a group of people to canvass in his city, to get signatures on a petition in favor of ratification.

And the girls who were with me, they canvassed door-to-door; worked just as hard as they could. It was less than a week we had to do it in. I especially went after prominent people. I mean the editor of the local newspaper, and clergymen, and prominent merchants in the town, and the women's clubs. We worked awfully hard that week, and finally on Saturday night we took the petitions up to the representative and left them with him. Well, then the state association, as they thought it over, decided the petition wasn't enough. They would like to have two people really go and talk with him and present the arguments, answer any objections he had, have the statistics and everything. So two women lawyers drove up on Sunday morning. They found him studying those petitions, and his eyes were fairly bugged out of his head when he saw the important people and the number of people we had gotten.

Well, they sat and they argued and they talked with him; he didn't commit himself. And his wife sat there in the room. She took no part in the conversation—she just heard everything that was discussed there. She sat there. And he wouldn't commit himself, but they finally left. And when the committee met on Monday, he swung it in favor of a favorable vote. The legislature followed the recommendation of the committee, and Massachusetts was one of the very early states that ratified. And it wasn't until later that we discovered that his wife had sat there listening to all this discussion, and had kept him awake practically all night arguing with him and urging him to vote in favor, to make his committee vote in favor.

The Postsuffrage Twenties

I enlisted in the suffrage fight while it still was a fight and an unpopular one. Now that the mantle of respectability has descended upon it I want to leave the work (great, patriotic, vitally important work as it is) for those who will do only the respectable things, and move on myself into the next fight of the future, which is not yet wholly proper. . . . I know in general it's the labor movement.

—Letter from Florence Luscomb to a friend on leaving the League of Women Voters, 1922.

With the vote won, the activity that had sustained the women's movement for so long disappeared. Feminists were unable to find another issue with the same kind of mass appeal. Disappointment was in store for those who had predicted that women would be an enormous voting bloc for social change. Women seemed to vote as conservatively as men, and as the nation moved into the twenties, the idealism of feminism of the earlier period was fading.

Florence Luscomb had worked almost exclusively in the suffrage movement since her teens and had not been directly involved in other kinds of political activism. But in campaigning for the vote, she had learned about the needs and problems of many different kinds of people. She met women laundry workers when she organized them for a 1915 suffrage parade; she had spoken with working men outside factory gates in open-air suffrage meetings. In the 1920s, Luscomb became involved in a broad range of social movements. She worked with the main successor to the suffrage movement, the League of Women Voters. She was also a member of the National Association for the Advancement of Colored People and worked in the women's peace movement. In the 1920 presidential election, Luscomb cast her first vote for Socialist party leader Eugene V. Debs. It was also during this period that Luscomb began working in the labor movement.

In the early twentieth century, hundreds of thousands of women worked in unsafe and low-paying jobs. In New York, for example, immigrants from southern and eastern Europe were shunted into garment sweatshops to turn out the ready-made clothing Americans were so eager to buy. There were no standards of cleanliness and no minimum hours in these shops, many of which were housed in the worst tenements of the city. In 1909, a small group of women workers at the Triangle Shirtwaist Company went out on strike to protest their working conditions and to establish a garment workers union. Joined by twenty thousand other garment workers in the dead of winter, they survived months of picketing and rent evictions. But when skilled male workers belonging to the conservative American Federation of Labor made separate agreements with ownership, the women lost their strike. In 1911, a horrible fire broke out in the very shop where the strike had started; the doors to the fire escapes were locked and 146 workers either jumped to their death from the upper story windows or were burned to death inside.

Some women of Luscomb's background were passionately concerned about the problems of women workers. They worked for minimum wage and maximum hour legislation and supported working-class women in their uphill battle with labor union leaders who ignored women's needs. These women—called social feminists—walked on picket lines with striking garment workers in 1909 and took in mill workers' children in the great Lawrence strike of 1912.[3] Hannah Luscomb worked in the Lawrence strike headquarters. It was after 1920, with the suffrage campaign over, that Florence Luscomb, too, joined in these kinds of struggles.

For political activists and working people, the decade following World War I was a difficult one. The International Ladies' Garment Workers' Union (ILGWU) emerged intact from the war. But the mill and garment shop owners in New England began moving their work south to take advantage of an un-unionized workforce, poor southern whites desperate for any kind of wages. These "runaway shops" made it hard for workers to maintain the gains made in the preceding decade. Many progressive and radical groups, including the Socialist party and the Industrial Workers of the World (IWW), were harassed by government officials, their offices and printing presses destroyed, their members tracked down in witch hunts.

Well, in all my work for suffrage, I got an education which I think was more basic than the things they teach you in colleges. I met and I swapped ideas with every kind of condition of men and women. It was a cross section of all humanity. The tragedy in the lives of most of us is that we go through life walking down a high-walled lane with people of our own kind, the same economic station, the same national background and education and religious outlook. And beyond those walls, all humanity lies, unknown and unseen, and untouched by our restricted and impoverished lives. Campaigning for "Votes for Women," talking with men and women of every kind, left my life mingled with the whole human race, and never again could I lose touch with humanity.

My life was especially enriched and broadened by certain contacts that I made. Very often we'd get an application from a Negro woman's club, church, or social club to have somebody come and talk to them about woman suffrage. And I was the person who was very often sent to speak to them. And waiting my turn to speak, I would be sitting there on the platform, and I'd be listening to all the business that they conducted in their meetings. I heard their reports of all the events and concerns of this Negro society. And I learned what most white people never heard, of the hideous injustices that were imposed on our black fellow citizens. I learned things that most people with white skin don't know. And then I was introduced, and I stood up to speak. For the first few minutes, I would be very, very conscious that my skin was white, and all the people I was watching were very dark. But it wasn't long before I became entirely unconscious that these faces were dark. They looked to me exactly like the other audiences that I had talked to. They were interested, this person was bored, that person was amused, over here was someone who was very enthusiastic and sympathetic with what I was saying. They were just like any other audience that I addressed, and I forgot there was any difference. And it was after one of these meetings that a woman came up to me, and she said, "There has just been organized an organization to fight for the rights of the black people." There'd been no organization in the whole country, up to that time, that had been struggling to remedy these injustices against the Negro. And she said, "Would you like to join this?" That was the National Association for the Advancement of Colored People, and I joined it on the spot. I was active in it, and some years later, I became vice-chairman of the local Boston branch of the NAACP.

As I burned with indignation at the injustices toward black Americans, I learned of a new organization that was founded in 1920 to defend the legal rights of all citizens, the American Civil Liberties Union. In addition to the bitter struggles of the black people, in the early part of this century, there were very bitter struggles of the working people against many illegal attacks and intolerable oppressions. The ACLU was defending these cases of labor, and so I joined the Massachusetts branch and was very active in it for many years. In fact, a short while later, I was made vice-chairman of it, and I served in that capacity for a good many years.

After the women got the vote in 1920, the suffrage association turned into the League of Women Voters, in order to provide civic leadership to the newly enfranchised women. It was at the last national convention in 1919, after the federal amendment had passed, but before it was ratified. I was a delegate to that convention in St. Louis, and Mrs. Carrie Chapman Catt, our great national president, got up and spoke to us. Mrs. Catt said, "This federal amendment that has just been passed by Congress will be ratified and go into effect within a year or two, and millions and millions of perfectly ignorant voters will come into the electorate. And you women here are the ones who are responsible for the great influx of ignorant voters. And," she said, "it is up to you to see to it that these women are educated and have leadership so that they use their vote for the things that we said we wanted women to be given the vote for: to get better schools, better health care, cleaner cities, better housing, more socially useful programs of our government." And the suffrage convention adjourned itself, and we convened on the spot as the founding convention for the League of Women Voters. For the first few years, the League of Women Voters did a magnificent work of education and leadership. I stayed on for a few years with the League of Women Voters. Then I went as assistant executive secretary to the Massachusetts Civic League. It was a group which worked for passage of legislation of a social welfare nature. And I stayed with them for two years. And the particular job that they took me on to do was to provide prisoners with pay for their work. Prisoners had to work, but they got no pay. When they were released from prison, many of them had not a penny in their pocket. So the Civic League felt they should have some financial remuneration for the work they were doing. Most of it would be piled up and given to them on their release, so that they would have a nest egg to live on until they could find a job. It was a pioneering bill—this hadn't been done anywhere. I was put in charge of trying to get it lobbied through the legislature. I had to write the leaflets explaining what it was and why it should be adopted, and then try to get important people to sponsor it, give their support to it, and bring it before all sorts of organizations. I had to go out and do speaking myself, or get other people to speak before all sorts of civic groups, and women's clubs, and what have you, and then arrange the hearing that was held on the bill. I was in charge of getting it through. And we got it through. The only thing was they earned a very, very low amount of money. But we'd broken the ice. We'd gotten it through, and in later years, they succeeded in raising the amount somewhat.

Then I was asked to come and be the executive secretary with the Joint Board of Sanitary Control. The International Ladies' Garment Workers' Union, in negotiating a union contract with the manufacturers of women's garments, had succeeded in getting them to agree to set up an inspection system of the safety and health conditions in the factories that were making women's garments. One of my friends had been the director of it, and had done the inspecting of the factories. Her husband got a job in New York, so the family was moving. She suggested me as her successor, and I was with the Joint Board of Sanitary Control for about two years. Of course, the state laws were supposed to guarantee decent and safe working conditions for the people in the factories. But the state inspection and enforcement of those laws was incredibly poor. And so the union felt that they wanted to have a supplementary inspection.

And again, I got an education as to what the conditions were of the working people. In those factories, I would find women sitting at a sewing machine with an electric light hanging down right in front of their eyes; the law required that it be shaded. There were certain parts of the moving machinery that were dangerous. If you caught your fingers in it, you might lose a finger. The law required that there should be guards around the dangerous parts of the machinery. But they didn't have them there. They required that the places be kept clean. I found they didn't bother to sweep up the floors, and they were littered with trash and bits of garbage. The law required that the doors of the factory be kept unlocked. A few years before there'd been a horrible fire, a hideous fire in New York, where the doors of the factory had been locked, and something over a hundred people were burned alive because there was no way they could escape. And I found exactly the same situation existing here in Boston— doors kept locked in violation of the law. And I would send in reports and complaints to the state inspection department, and they paid no attention to my complaints as to what I had found there. So one time I got four of the most socially prominent women in Boston, who had some public spirit and interest, and I got them to go with me on an inspection trip. I showed them what there was in these factories. They were indignant at what they saw, and they wrote up a report of the conditions. We sent it, not only to the state department, but we sent it to the newspapers, and the newspapers printed it over the names of these important Back Bay residents of Boston. And believe me, the state department came down and cleaned up those factories within twenty-four hours!

Well, about this time, the union was getting weaker here in Boston, because a good many of the shops were moving to the far South, where they could get non-union labor at very much lower pay. So the union was not strong enough, when the contract expired, to insist on the continuation of the Joint Board of Sanitary Control, and it was done away with. So then I took a job, this was in the late 1920s, with the Women's International League for Peace and Freedom. I was the executive secretary for Massachusetts until 1933, and that was the last paid job I've held.

The WILPF was a pioneering organization in the field of peace. One of the outstanding founders of it was Jane Addams. It grew out of a woman's movement in the First World War. The members were feminists in the sense that they felt that women should organize as women to continue their activities against war. They felt that all the pressure women could bring for peace and for setting up international institutions would help to keep peace. They were trying to build up the popular belief that all international disputes should be settled without war, that they should be settled through the League of Nations and an international court. They opposed the building up of large armies, large military appropriations, and any imperialist action by this government.

The WILPF was having its annual convention, and they asked each of the local branches to make suggestions for resolutions to be adopted. And so our local branch, in a board meeting, talked over what different subjects we would like to suggest that they take actions on. And after we decided this, they parceled them out to each one of us to draft the resolution to send on to the national. I was given the one to draft about the power of the munitions industry over national policies. And, as I started to draft it, I realized that I couldn't prove any of those charges. I couldn't denounce them for it, because we didn't know any of the facts. So all I could draft was a resolution asking that Congress investigate, set up an investigation of the power of the munitions industry over government policies. So I drafted it that way, and the board sent it on to the national convention, and the national convention adopted it. And that meant that the national office had to try to implement that. The national executive secretary, Dorothy Detzer, did the lobbying, and she tried to get some congressmen to introduce a resolution to have such an investigation made. She got Congressman Gerald P. Nye to, and Congress passed it. As is customary, the congressman who introduces a resolution which is adopted calling for an investigation is made chairman of the committee of investigation. So Nye was head of the congressional committee which carried this investigation. And they brought in a very fine report, with very substantial facts to back them up. But that's how it came about that I am responsible for the Nye investigation of the munitions industry![4]

The New Spirit of the Thirties

How well do I remember how class
  struggle brought me through,
I went out on strike in nineteen-thirty-two.

They brought the thugs against me
  and the state militia, too,

And they kicked me in the gutter,
  How about you!

We need a brand new system, that's
  one thing that is true,
The boss will have to work like me and you.

We'll all have homes to live in, and
  a job to work at, too,
But there'll be no boss to rob us,
  Me and you.

—*Song by Jim Garland, 1932.*

In 1929, the Great Depression began; it would last a decade. By 1933, nearly a quarter of all Americans were without jobs. Hundreds of thousands lost their homes because they were evicted or could not keep up mortgage payments. While industrial collapse brought distress to millions in the cities, agricultural disaster ravaged the countryside, as teeming dust storms swept the lower Midwest. Farm families, driven from their homes, crammed possessions into battered cars and roamed the country in search of work. Tens of thousands of teen-agers and adults rode the rails looking for jobs and shelter.

While the Franklin D. Roosevelt administration launched public works programs and took other measures to get the economy moving again, conditions for most people ranged from difficult to disastrous. Yet these very conditions sparked one of the most exciting decades in the history of United States labor organizing. In nearly every industry, new unions sprang up to challenge the leadership of the American Federation of Labor, which had long neglected the organization of industrial, unskilled, immigrant, Afro-American, and women workers. The AF of L also ignored the unemployed. The new, young labor movement that opposed the AF of L swept the coal mines, the automobile plants, the steel mills, the textile mills, the docks, and the merchant marine. The new unions that emerged in these areas of work combined in 1936 to form the Congress of Industrial Organizations.

Thousands of young people pitched themselves into the battle of "organizing the unorganized," as the CIO described its goal. The CIO led strikes in automobile plants in Detroit, halted coal mining in Kentucky, and closed down the docks to gain union recognition and more reasonable working conditions. Throughout this period, the Communist party of the United States provided much of the most effective leadership in labor struggles, and many young people joined the Party because of this. The Party encouraged alliances with non-Communist trade union organizers in the CIO, organizers of poor southern farmworkers, and others. They called the forming of such alliances "the popular front."

A. J. Muste, a famous peace activist, worked in the radical labor movement in the 1930s. He later said of the Communists, "When you looked out on the scene of misery and desperation during the Depression, you saw that it was the radicals, the Left-wingers, the people who had adopted some form of Marxian philosophy, who were *doing something* about the situation. . . . Unless you were indifferent or despairing, you lined up with them."[5] Through the Communist party, people saw visions of a new society in the Soviet Union, where revolution had taken place a little over a decade before.[6] They looked with hope to a revolutionary struggle being born in China.

Florence Luscomb speaks of the Party. She never joined it, for, as she explains, she did not agree with some of its policies. One Communist party policy that Luscomb strongly opposed was its support of a no-strike pledge. Once the Soviet Union had entered World War II, the Party became a staunch supporter of the American war effort and wanted nothing to interfere with the fight to save the Soviet Union and defeat fascism. It encouraged CIO unions to honor a no-strike pledge so that production for the war effort would be uninterrupted.[7]

During the 1930s, there was no ongoing feminist movement.[8] Many young women who would have joined the feminist movement in an earlier decade probably joined the Communist party or became union organizers instead. However, neither the Communist party nor the CIO unions worked particularly hard for women. Although theoretically concerned about "the woman question," in practice, the Communist party had very few high ranking women Party officials. Women generally were expected to take care of house and family—even if they were Party workers as well. On the other hand, in the very ways in which they were vigorously leading social movements, young Communist women belied the traditional image of the passive female.

The CIO unions, if they organized women, usually did so as an afterthought. Since women were a large sector of the garment, textile, and packing house industries, they came into these unions. But the major objective of the CIO was to organize the large basic industries, which usually had few women workers. While the CIO leadership did not object to organizing waitresses, retail clerks, or laundry workers, these major areas of employment for women were not made special targets of union work. By the mid-thirties, clerical work was the third most likely occupation for women. Yet the CIO union for clerical workers, the United Office and Professional Workers of America, lumped office workers in with other white-collar workers like insurance agents and social workers.

In the thirties, Luscomb worked to organize clerical workers into the UOPWA. But, as she found, there were many obstacles in the pathway of this work. The professional organizers sent by the national office of the union often ignored the clerical workers and focused on insurance salesmen, bank tellers, and publishing editors. Other union organizers—including some of the most radical ones, who were often Communists—believed that all white-collar workers were privileged middle-class people, and that less effort should be put into organizing them than into organizing blue-collar workers. That women clerical workers in the 1930s were likely to earn a subsistence wage no higher than factory workers, that they were often from immigrant and working-class families, was frequently ignored.

In fact, office workers, themselves, sometimes felt better off than their sisters working in factories. The relative cleanliness and safety of office work and the opportunity to dress up contributed to these perceptions. For many immigrant families, a daughter who had graduated high school and who worked in an office represented social prestige, despite low wages. Women office workers often worked in small groups and were usually isolated from each other. All these factors made organizing clerical workers difficult. But often radical organizers focused on these problems so much that they became self-fulfilling prophecies, and any potential for clerical worker militancy was overlooked.

Hannah Luscomb died in 1933, and Florence went through a rocky period as she adjusted to life without her mother. In 1935, she visited the Soviet Union and came home exhilarated by the progress she felt she had seen there. Having inherited a comfortable sum of money from her mother's estate, she never had a paid job again. Instead, she worked as a volunteer; she felt guilty earning a salary when others were suffering so much. Her old friend from suffrage days, Zara duPont, moved to Cambridge, and the two women became familiar figures on local picket lines. Many of the young women active in the local UOPWA became her camping and mountain climbing companions, and in 1939, Luscomb built her small log cabin in Tamworth, New Hampshire, open every summer to friends who wanted to visit.

During the Great Depression, there were a great many strikes in the labor movement, and I went out on picket lines whenever they had a strike anywhere. I picketed with the International Ladies' Garment Workers, with the Amalgamated Clothing Workers, with the Teamsters' Union, with the National Maritime Union. I also raised a lot of money for the National Maritime, when they had a strike, and they made me an honorary member of the union.

I've been ridden down by mounted cops who were breaking up a perfectly legal picket line. One time, over in Everett, there was an oil tanker at port there, and the workers went out on strike against the company. The workers set up a picket line, and the police broke up that picket line by hurling tear gas at it. Now mind you, the law said that a picket line, a peaceful picket line, was legal. And the police hurled tear gas at that line to break it up so that the scabs could go through for the company.* But it

---

* A scab (also called a strikebreaker) is a worker who agrees to work in a place that is being struck by other workers. The power of a strike is in withholding the labor of a company's workers, and hence, the company's ability to produce its goods. If enough scabs go to work, that ability to produce won't be weakened, and the strike will be defeated, or "broken."

so happened that there was a breeze blowing sideways, and it blew that tear gas through a wire fence and onto a playground for children at Everett. And half a dozen of the children were so seriously affected that many of them had to be rushed off to the hospital! Well, the night that the police had used the tear gas, the union got in touch with Miss duPont and myself. They asked us if we would go out on the picket line the next morning wearing gas masks so that all the people would know what was being done to the strikers. So we went over there, and when you get a duPont family member wearing a gas mask in a picket line, it makes some sensation and goes all over the country. And then the fact that the children had been gassed made a terrific outburst from the citizens in Everett, and they had an official investigation of the use of gas by the police against a legal picket line. It was revealed that the police were not only being paid by the city, but they were on the payroll of the shipping company, with the knowledge and approval of the chief of police!

Then I was ten months on the picket line of a little strike over in Cambridge, at the Martin Moving Firm. It was right next to the police headquarters that's right there in Central Square. And one of the girls who belonged to our Office and Professional Workers' Union happened to be passing by one day and saw these picket lines, and she stopped and asked them about it. They said they worked terribly hard all day lugging furniture and they got very low pay. There was a state law for safety in driving —if you had a man you hired to drive a truck, you couldn't work him more than, say, ten hours a day. So Martin's men would start at six in the morning. He'd work them about ten hours, and then if he had a load, he'd start them off driving to New York. So they'd just get over the state line within the limit of the ten hours, and they'd still have to drive all these other hours, exhausted, after a terrifically hard day's work beforehand. He got the overtime work out of them and got around the state law. Well, three of the men began talking to their fellow workers about setting up a union, and getting decent pay and decent working conditions. Martin heard of it, and he fired these three. They started picketing in front of his headquarters, and there

(text continued on page 40)

Making History

Florence Luscomb, now in her nineties, has spent over seventy years organizing for social change. She has worked—with countless other dedicated women and men—in the labor, suffrage, peace, and contemporary women's movements. **1:** May Day parade, 1936. **2:** Women's International League for Peace and Freedom, 1914. **3:** Executive Committee of the International Council of Women, July 5, 1899; Susan B. Anthony, front row, third from left. **4:** Sweatshop workers in New York City, c. 1911. **5:** Organizing for suffrage. **6:** Labor march. **7:** Women's Day march, Boston, 1976. **8:** International Women's Year Conference, Houston, Texas, November 1977.

37

were just these three men to picket. All the others were still working. This girl who brought up the news about it said they needed help on the picket line, so some of us went over there and picketed. I went over, and Zara picketed too, every morning at six. Of course, after the trucks had gone, there wasn't much point in picketing a vacant garage. But for an hour or two in the morning we'd picket, and day after day we did, all through some difficult winter and some hot summer days.

I joined the American Federation of Labor, what they called the Stenographers, Typewriters, Bookkeepers, and Accountants Union. Not typists, but typewriters. I joined it in the early thirties, because I believed in labor unions, and so I wanted to be a member. And it was really just a fake union. There was just this one public stenographers' office in Boston, and that was a union office. The woman who ran this office and one of the labor men who was a great friend of hers were running this union. When I became president in 1936, I wanted to put on a big campaign to unionize more office workers. And they wouldn't do it. The reason they wouldn't do it was because they were the only union public stenographers in Boston. There were all sorts of other labor unions that couldn't afford to hire permanent stenographers themselves, but had to have the union label on all their things, so they had to come and have their work done at this one office. And if there'd been other union public stenographic offices, why they'd have lost some of their trade. They wouldn't put on a real campaign to get big unionization for them, so I was not very much interested in that union. When the Congress of Industrial Organizations came along and started to establish a United Office and Professional Workers' Union, they called a convention, and I went down to that convention. And the union was established. Then we came back to Boston and got together various other people, and we set up local No. 3 of the UOPWA in the CIO. I was the president for several years, and we did a lot of very active work without getting a very large union.

For example, there was one big firm which had quite a large office staff, and they paid very low wages. We used to go around and find one girl in the office who would think that they ought to be organized, and she'd give us the names and addresses of all the office workers. We'd go and visit them in their homes, and talk union with them. And we got a large group of girls in this office who were very much interested in having the union there. The firm got wind of it, that they were probably going to have a strike on their hands. So they raised their girls' pay, whereupon the girls lost all interest in joining the union! And that happened various times. We got more stenographers with pay raises than we got members of the union, but we did gradually build up the union. It was a new idea for office workers to organize—it was a very unusual idea. They felt themselves socially superior to the person working in a factory, although they might get much less pay than the girls who were working in the factory. The CIO didn't give much assistance in having secretaries organized; they'd be too busy trying to organize the textile workers, and the railroad workers, and large "important" bodies of the working class.

In 1936, a lot of the labor people and left-wingers were trying to see what would be the chance of establishing a radical or progressive party here. They wanted to try out a candidate running for Congress as an independent, but having the support of a lot of individual labor leaders. So they asked me to do it, and they called it the People's Labor ticket. I ran, that was in 1936, in the Ninth Congressional district. But they didn't make enough of a success of it. I mean nothing permanent came out of it.

I didn't ever seriously consider joining the Communist party. I'll tell you why. I've always had a great many Communist friends, and Socialist friends, and they're all on good terms with me. But I felt that several of the policies and the strategies of the Communist party were very poor, very wrong, very mistaken. So if you joined the Communist party, you had no choice, you had to follow. The orders came down from the Central Committee as to what should be the policies, and you had to accept it exactly. And I couldn't do that on all the things.

For example, during World War II, organized labor pledged not to go on any strikes; they would have maximum production during the war. I was a member of a trade union, the UOPWA, and as the war was coming to a close, the Communist party decided that they would continue that pledge. They would ask every union where they had strong representation to try to get that local union to pass a resolution asking the CIO to renew this pledge of no strikes. So they brought it up in my local. And I got up and I said that I lived through the First World War, and I knew that immediately after the war there was the great witch hunt, and they started to smash all the unions. So I said, there is every likelihood that the same thing will be done, that the powers that be will make this attack and destroy organized labor. And you want them to pledge that they won't go on strike! So one of the Communists who wanted us to pass this resolution said, "Oh, all we mean is that if they don't attack us, we won't attack them." And one of the girls who belonged to the union, but who didn't realize that this was the Communists who were trying to get this thing through, got up and said, "Well, if that's what we mean, isn't that what we should say in the resolution?" So I immediately moved that that be the form in which we would phrase our resolution, and they had to pass it that way in our local. But they were getting that other thing passed in locals all over the country where they had a large number of Communist members.

A New Witch Hunt

I stated in the beginning that I knew of no one among my personal acquaintances who was subversive. I do know of subversion abroad in our land. It is subversive to set up inquisitions like this, state or national, into the thoughts and consciences of Americans, into their speeches, their writings, their associations one with another, their political activities. It is subversive to starve Americans by throwing them out of jobs because of their opinions. It is subversive to blast careers and lives of scientists and professors, writers and artists, doctors and medical researchers, and rob America of the priceless contributions they could have made to our national welfare. It is subversive for commissions like this, some of whose members claim to be pro-labor, to conspire with big corporations to attack labor just when negotiations are pending, to divide and wreck the union. It is subversive for commissions like this to spread such hysteria and intimidation throughout the land that Americans are afraid to sign petitions, afraid to read progressive magazines, afraid to make out checks for liberal causes, afraid to join organizations, afraid to speak their minds on public issues. Americans dare not be free citizens! This is the destruction of democracy.

—Statement by Florence Luscomb to the Commission to Investigate Communism in Massachusetts, January 7, 1955.

Luscomb's fear of another period of political repression after World War II proved to be prophetic. Conservative Republicans made steady gains in Congress during the forties, and in 1947, Congress passed the Taft-Hartley Act, giving the federal government the right to intervene in labor disputes and order strikers back to work. The House Un-American Activities Committee, which had originally been organized in 1938 by political conservatives to heckle the Congress of Industrial Organizations and the New Deal, resumed hearings. It was soon making inflammatory headlines, as it badgered men and women who had worked in liberal and left-wing causes in the thirties about their alleged Communist associations. Ambitious, unscrupulous politicians like Richard Nixon and Joseph McCarthy, then Senator from Wisconsin, made fame for themselves as they "discovered Communists under every bed." To be a radical, a socialist, or a Communist party member in the forties and fifties in the United States was to be "red-baited": relentlessly attacked by Nixon, McCarthy, and others. The nets of anti-Communist hysteria were cast wide. In every institution— schools, universities, the film industry, labor unions, publishing—committees were set up to track down "reds." Luscomb saw many of her friends expelled from organizations to which they had belonged for years. She saw them lose their jobs; she saw them go to jail. Liberals in the CIO, fearful that they would be attacked next, and anxious for complete control over the union leadership, began expelling Communist organizers and the unions in which the Communist party had influence. The United Office and Professional Workers, which had included Party members, was kicked out of the CIO in 1950, and the organization of clerical workers came to a halt.

The witch hunt was part of a larger United States policy. The end of World War II was the beginning of a "cold war" aggressively pursued by the United States. Under President Harry Truman, United States foreign policy systematically attacked communism in America's erstwhile wartime ally, the Soviet Union; in China; in long-established Communist parties in Western Europe. The witch hunt within the United States was the cold war's guarantee of keeping the American people afraid of worldwide revolutionary movements that had inspired radical activity in this country from the late nineteenth century on. United States foreign policy was the cold war's worldwide arm, through which it launched covert attacks on left-leaning governments around the world.

It took courage to oppose the cold war. Yet some Americans tried to continue the social movements of the thirties after World War II. They banded together in 1947 to form the Progressive party, protested against the proliferation of nuclear weapons, and continued to support labor organizing in the face of the Taft-Hartley Act, which helped turn unions in this country into bastions of conservatism. They opposed the maintaining and extension of American military bases in Europe. They urged Truman to move away from his position of adamant hostility toward the Soviet Union. In 1948, the Progressive party ran a presidential candidate, Henry Wallace. Even after Wallace left the Progressive party, it was sustained in some communities and it launched a criticism of the growing American presence in Southeast Asia. Luscomb ran for governor of Massachusetts on the Progressive party ticket in 1952. In 1954, she composed the first leaflet against the Vietnam war to be distributed in Boston.

Red-baited herself, Luscomb raised money for the defense of victims of the witch hunt.[9] She spent the decade of the fifties doing that, protesting the spread of nuclear weapons, and fighting for better race relations. Avidly, she followed the progress of the Chinese revolution, about which she had first read in 1937. The forties and the fifties were unhappy decades for many activists, but Luscomb tried to connect herself with whatever progressive movements she could find. By the 1960s, she found new hope in a new generation of student activists, in the civil rights and peace movements, and in the fruition of the Chinese revolution.

In 1948, there was a Progressive party campaign, running Henry Wallace as its candidate. I was the director of the campaign for the state of Maine. I was active in the Progressive party in Boston, and the different states were having conventions. The state of Maine wanted to have such a convention, but they didn't feel that they knew how to organize it. So they wrote down to Massachusetts, and said could they send somebody to help them get up this first convention—somebody who would know how to organize it. They asked me to go. I was there for three or four weeks, getting the convention going, and they asked would I stay on and be the campaign manager for the state. It might have gone on, and grown, but Henry Wallace didn't stick by it. You see, that was in the campaign of '48. In '50, we went into Korea, and the Progressive party denounced our going into Korea to fight. And the party morale just disintegrated, although it lasted for quite a number of years after that. I ran once or twice on the Progressive ticket—for Congress in 1950 and for governor of Massachusetts in 1952.

About thirty years ago, Edgar Snow wrote Red Star over China, and I read it as soon as it came out.* And I was terrifically interested in it, and from that time on, I bought every book that was published here, in America, on China. That isn't as exciting as it sounds, because it was about one or two books a year. I kept myself informed on the history of the Chinese Liberation struggle. So I really had kept in touch with the defeat of Chiang Kai-shek and his whole corrupt regime.

Well, for my seventy-fifth birthday, quite a large number of my friends contributed to give me as a present a trip to Japan to attend the conference against atomic and hydrogen bombs that they hold there every year. And then I discovered that the cost of going to Japan and back was only two hundred dollars less than a trip around the world! In the same year, the World Council of Peace was having a conference in Moscow, so I made up my mind I would go around the world, and attend the Mos-

* Edgar Snow was a young journalist from Kansas City who journeyed to the Red Army headquarters in northwestern China in 1936 to interview Communist party leaders and observe the areas under their influence. His vivid and enthusiastic description of the revolution, Red Star over China, published in 1937, remains a classic. He and Anna Louise Strong were the first Western journalists to meet and interview Mao Tse Tung.

cow conference, and then go on to Tokyo for the other one. There was no direct transportation from Moscow to Tokyo—the ordinary route was you flew down through India, and then up around through Hong Kong and Tokyo. I made up my mind that instead of going that way, I would go down through China. But in this country, I had no way of arranging a visa. I couldn't apply to the Chinese consulate here, or anything. So when I got to the Moscow conference, I hunted out the Chinese delegation that had come to the Moscow conference, and I asked them if they could get me a visa to go down through China. There were about a dozen of the American delegates there who were also asking for visas from China. Well, the Chinese had been welcoming people from every country on earth except Americans. They didn't want to get in spies and saboteurs. They wanted to know who the people were that they were letting in from the United States. So they submitted all of these dozen names to Anna Louise Strong, who was then living in Peking. She always went to the countries where they had revolutionary movements, where the peoples' movements were developing. She went into the Soviet Union many, many years ago, and then she went there and lived for many years. She married a Russian. And he died during the war, but she lived there and edited a newspaper. So she came back to this country and was on lecture tours, and she was speaking in Boston, and I presided at the meeting. I put her up in my house when she was here. I can't say that we were friends, but we had met. And that was why, when I asked for a visa, she remembered me, and vouched that I was not a member of the CIA. So they gave me a visa. They gave a visa to one other woman whose daughter had married a Chinese student when he was over here and had gone back to China with him. The mother hadn't seen her daughter for seventeen years, and had never seen her grandchildren, so it was perfectly obvious why she wanted to go to China. And they were willing to give a visa to another woman who had done a great deal of work in the international peace movement. But she thought it over, and she finally decided that the United States government might take away her passport, and it might interfere with her international peace work.

The China Peace Committee provided me with guides and interpreters in each of the cities. And I worked day and night. The first thing they'd do when I went to a place was, they'd say, well, what do you want to see? And they'd show me the things that I knew about. I knew that Shanghai had been the only place before the liberation that had any industry at all, so I said I'd like to see a big factory. I knew that Shanghai was running neck-and-neck with Tokyo to be the biggest city in the world, about ten million population. And Shanghai had decided that they weren't going to have the city grow anymore, and instead they were leaving a green belt around the city and starting new industries in what they called satellite cities. They would take me to see everything I asked to see, and then they would show me all the rest of the things that I hadn't known enough to ask.

I think the Chinese Revolution is the most important revolution, for several reasons. In the first place, it affects a quarter of the human race. China's population is a quarter of all humanity. That's basic, isn't it? Then the fact that China was so far back, the conditions of the people—the illiteracy among the peasants was 90 percent. Only the wealthy families, and only the men in the wealthy families by and large, had any education at all. At the liberation, China had a population of somewhere between four hundred and five hundred million, and they had twenty-five thousand doctors. The new government immediately started training doctors, and in '63 they graduated twenty-five thousand doctors that one year. And then they were instituting the system of training what they called the "barefoot doctors," from the villages, giving them six months basic training so that they could diagnose diseases. They knew how to treat the simple ones, and they'd know which ones needed to be sent to the central hospital.

If you know anything about the condition of women in China throughout history, you know that they were utterly oppressed. A girl was sold into marriage, often as a child. She would become the domestic slave in her husband's family, to toil at domestic tasks, to be a servant for her mother-in-law. The husband could beat her, he could give her away, he could sell her, he could kill her. It was his legal right, it wasn't a crime. When she got old, if she got to be the matriarch of the family, then she had considerable importance, but only within the walls of the home, only in the family affairs. One of the first laws that the new government promulgated after they came into power, after liberation in '49, was to declare the full equality of women in every way. Marriage was to take place only by the agreement of the young couple themselves. The women would have equal ownership in land, in the communes, or in their little private plots. Women were elected to public office. When I was there the number of women who were members of the national Congress was 18 percent, which is a vastly greater number than our Congress. When I was in Peking, I asked to be taken to Peking University. And then as a good feminist, I asked them how many of the students were girls. And they said that 28 percent of the students were girls. And then they hastened to add, "But you understand that in the olden days, the girls did not get any education, and so a larger number were not qualified to enter college. But just give us a few years, and you'll find that it'll be 50–50." Now you can't change the whole thinking of people by passing a law, and there are undoubtedly many of the older people who still look upon women as inferiors. But women have been taking their active part in all the public affairs.

Final Reflections

Until all . . . discriminations against women are done away with, I won't say that I'm satisfied with the condition of women.

—From a speech by Florence Luscomb at the University of Rhode Island, May 3, 1973.

In the early seventies, Florence Luscomb was discovered by the current women's movement. She had long been active in the antiwar movement. She had given dozens of talks at demonstrations, classes, and meetings. She still works a certain amount of time each week as a volunteer to the Massachusetts Women's International League for Peace and Freedom. She contributes much of her small income to legal defense funds and radical organizations. She has lived in cooperatives in and around Cambridge since the middle fifties and has always done her share of the cooking and cleaning. She says now that she is an avowed communist; that is, while not belonging to any particular political party, she believes that social revolution should come to the United States, and that workers should control the means of production.

Young women often want to know why Florence Luscomb has never married. For Luscomb's generation, marrying or not marrying meant choosing a certain path in life and giving up other options. By marrying, a woman almost certainly gave up a career outside the home. By not marrying, a woman generally gave up the lifetime companionship of a male partner and probably gave up having children. In these last passages, Florence Luscomb talks about her political beliefs, her feminism, and her decision not to marry.

I would have liked to be married, if I had found the man that I loved. I have many, many good friends who are men. But I never met one of them that I wanted to spend my life with, and ever wanted to marry. And I would much rather go through life unmarried, than get married just for the sake of being married.

I was the third generation of the woman's movement. You folks are the fifth generation in this great, tremendous historical movement affecting half the human race. And there are still some very serious changes that need to be made. We've spoken about equal pay for equal work, and equal opportunity in the industrial field, and in the professional world, too. We need the child-care centers to make women free to go out into society and use their talents. We are beginning to realize that women should have the choice as to how many, and when, she will bear children. Personally, I resent the fact that when a woman gets married, she takes her husband's name. I think it is an invasion of one's personality to have your name taken away from you. A woman becomes Mrs. John Smith; can you imagine having the boy, when he got married, Mr. Mary Jones? That's exactly what happens to women! I think women have got to be less dependent on fashion and cosmetics and all of those outward appearances. There are probably other things that need changing, but these are the basic changes that still remain to be mopped up. And I think, I always feel very sure of this, that men are going to be very great gainers in this. They're going to get a comradeship out of their women, in their contacts with women, that they don't get when they think of women as inferiors. And when women are working side by side with them on all the great public issues, and carrying on the life of humanity, I think that men are going to get comradeship that only the really advanced men have now. And when we have amended the Declaration of Independence so that it reads, "All men and women are created equal," this new force of men and women will be able to go forward and create a society of peace and of social justice and of beauty we haven't ever known in this world.

Of course, I am an avowed socialist. The reason, for example, for much of the discrimination against women in employment —that they don't get equal pay even when they do the same work that a man does, and that they don't get promoted to the better paid, more responsible, and more interesting jobs—is that under a capitalist society, owners of the factories can make money by having this large body of workers that they can pay less money to. When business is run solely for profit, naturally they're going to try to maintain a group of cheap labor.

I have come face-to-face with the question, "Is America still a democracy? Is it ruled by the people, by their votes?" And I have been forced to answer, "No." Behind the screen of the ballot, the real holders of power who decide national policies and laws, and control public opinion by their ownership of all the mass media of information are the great industrial and monetary monopolies who own our national economic life. They, together with the armed forces—the military industrial complex—are the real rulers of our country today. The outstanding example is the undeniable fact that the American people never decided to intervene in the civil war in distant Vietnam. Actually, most Americans never heard of Vietnam when we went in there. The military industrial complex saw vast profits that they could make from armaments and from gaining a controlling foothold in the natural resources and economy of Southeast Asia, and so America went to war in Vietnam. The Watergate affair is another example of the loss of democracy here. America is a capitalist society. Capitalism, by definition, sets money as the sole mode of power which keeps us running. Every man for himself. From my lifetime experiences, I have reached the firm conviction that the only possible basis for a successful, just, and peaceful world society is a cooperative economy of production for human needs, not for individual profits. That is the basic principle of communism.

I'll tell you the way I feel about it. I think that the world is in one of the great transition ages when we are moving from a capitalist to a socialist-communist world. And that takes maybe a hundred years, or maybe two hundred years, it's not a thing that happens overnight.

I don't get depressed. I am to do what I can for the triumph of the policies that I believe in. It's my job to work, to try to see that right prevails. I often make this comparison. There is nothing in the world that is so transitory and fragile as a snow-flake, and there is nothing so irresistible as an avalanche, which is simply millions of snowflakes. So that if each one of us, little snowflakes, just does our part, we will be an irresistible force.

TWO:
Ella Baker

Organizing for Civil Rights

By Ellen Cantarow and Susan Gushee O'Malley

ELLA BAKER IS A behind-the-scenes activist; one of the great organizers of the past fifty years. When the Reverend Martin Luther King founded a new civil rights organization in 1957 with other ministers, he called on Ella Baker to set up the organization's national office and organize its mass meetings. She remembers: "I set up the office of the Southern Christian Leadership Conference in 1958, but you didn't see me on television, you didn't see news stories about me. The kind of role that I tried to play was to pick up pieces or put together pieces out of which I hoped organization might come. My theory is, strong people don't need strong leaders."

CHRONOLOGY

1903: Ella Baker born, Norfolk, Virginia, to Georgianna and Blake Baker.

1911: Moves to Littleton, North Carolina, where grandparents bought and lived on land they had worked as slaves.

1918–27: Attends secondary school and college at Shaw University in Raleigh, North Carolina. Graduates from Shaw.

1927–29: Moves to New York City and lives with cousin. Does waitressing and some factory work. The Depression begins.

1929–30: Editorial staff member of *American West Indian News*.

1932: Office manager and editorial assistant for *Negro National News*. Becomes national director of the Young Negroes' Cooperative League and also works on WPA consumer education project.

1938: Begins working with the National Association for the Advancement of Colored People.

1943: Named national director of branches of the NAACP, where she emphasizes job training for black workers.

1946: Takes on responsibility for raising her niece.

1954: The Supreme Court rules segregation in public schools unconstitutional. Ella Baker becomes president of the New York City branch of the NAACP. To support herself, she works for the New York Cancer Society.

1958: Serves as executive secretary of the Southern Christian Leadership Conference and works with Martin Luther King.

1960: Helps found the Student Nonviolent Coordinating Commitee. Works for the YWCA in Atlanta as a consultant in human relations.

1964: Mississippi Freedom Democratic Party organized. Baker keynotes MFDP's Jackson convention and sets up the Washington office.

1967: Joins the Southern Conference Educational Fund staff.

1972–present: Vice-chairperson of the Mass Party Organizing Committee. National board member of the Puerto Rican Solidarity Committee. Serves as an advisor to numerous human rights and liberation groups.

The woman who has just spoken is seated on a couch in a modest apartment in Harlem. What is striking about the apartment is the quantities of newspapers, pamphlets, books, and magazines that surround its inhabitant. Much of the literature is about black American and African history. Ella Baker herself is in her seventies. She is slight and wiry, with a finely chiseled, expressive, beautiful face. Her voice projects way beyond her size. It has terrific force, depth, and variety. Its inflections can change from seriousness to wry humor to matter-of-factness within the turn of a sentence. Often it breaks into deep laughter. It mimics a stuffy professor, mocks a snobbish social climber in that offender's own cadences. Throughout, it is a very southern voice, despite its owner's many years in New York City. It is almost the voice of an actress or orator, except that Ella Baker is the opposite of anything staged or self-important. We—two young women who've come announced only by the purpose of what we are writing—come as strangers. She receives us as friends, and she shares her life with us. What she tells us explains the roots of her conviction that a political activist must work to build strong people, not strong leaders.

Ella Baker was born in Norfolk, Virginia, and grew up in rural North Carolina where she received her formal education, graduating from Shaw University in Raleigh. Her grandfather, who had been a slave, was a minister who seated his granddaughter before the congregation, in a big chair beside his own. He called her "Grand Lady." Her father worked as a waiter on a ferry that ran between Norfolk and Washington. Baker's mother was a strong woman. She cared for the ill and needy of the community; she was the sort of woman people went to for help and advice. She was also "a hard taskmaster." A "stickler for grammar," she wanted her children to speak beautifully and to go to college. Baker's earliest ambition was to be a medical missionary, and once at Shaw, she considered becoming a sociologist.

The family wasn't poor, but it also wasn't one of means—particularly in the late twenties, just before the Great Depression broke. In 1927, Baker moved to New York City where she had relatives. There she became active in a consumers' rights movement. She also joined and worked for the National Association for the Advancement of Colored People (NAACP). She traveled around the South, talking about pressing issues—police brutality, unequal salaries between blacks and whites. She urged people to join the NAACP. She solicited money. In 1942, the NAACP leadership made Baker national director of all the organization's local branches. Later, she served as president of the NAACP's New York chapter and worked on school desegregation.

From 1958 to 1960, Baker worked for the Southern Christian Leadership Conference (SCLC). In 1960, she helped found the Student Nonviolent Coordinating Committee (SNCC, pronounced "Snick"). It was an organization established to coordinate the thousands of black southern students who had begun sitting in at lunch counters and other public places, and who had begun conducting mass, peaceful demonstrations to break the back of southern segregation. In 1964, Baker helped found the Mississippi Freedom Democratic Party, which would challenge the racism of the mainstream party at the 1964 Democratic convention. In the sixties, she was also on the staff of the Southern Conference Educational Fund (SCEF). From the mid-sixties through the present, she has lived in a small apartment in Harlem, where mail arrives continuously to request her services as a consultant for human rights organizations and as a speaker at meetings and rallies.

Roots

I woke up this morning with my mind
  Stayed on freedom,
I woke up this morning with my mind
  Stayed on freedom,
I woke up this morning with my mind
  Stayed on freedom,
Hallelu, Hallelu, Hallelu, Hallelu, Hallelujah!

—*Traditional hymn, sung as a civil rights song in the sixties.*

Ella Baker grew up hearing her grandparents talk about slavery. The very North Carolina soil on which the family lived—Baker and her parents moved there from Norfolk, Virginia, when she was eight—was a tribute to dignity. It signified, concretely, that Ella Baker's grandfather had taken back turf rightfully his through his toil. He bought the land on which he had slaved. Once it was his, he worked it for no master. He and Baker's grandmother made it yield abundance for their family and the surrounding community. Her grandmother was a determined, independent woman. A photograph shows her seated, strong-looking, holding against her a child who is shrinking back shyly from the photographer. One of Ella Baker's earliest memories is of being chased, with her cousins, to the threshold of her grandmother's kitchen by a cow who hated children. Once at the threshold, the cow was stopped by Baker's grandmother, who stood in the doorway brandishing a broom while the children rushed over the sill and behind her.

Food, cooking, a garden plot, a kitchen. They appear and reappear in Ella Baker's story of her growing up. As she speaks, everyday things take on a larger meaning. In them are the roots of future beliefs and work.

When I was about seven or eight, we would go to grandpa's every summer. He believed in the old pattern of providing. He had developed an orchard with multiple, rare, and a variety of fruits—the seasoning and the stages and the ripening and the like. He insisted on having plenty to eat, which meant that he always had milk by the gallons. And he did not believe in eating certain things that he had eaten during slavery. He could not eat corn bread as such. You see, there is a corn bread that you make just by putting water into the cornmeal. Which is just plain. I'm sure that the slaves did not enjoy the privilege of egg bread— we called it egg bread growing up.* This he would eat, but he would not eat the other. He wouldn't let his wife even force the children to eat the corn bread. He was a great hunter, or trapper rather, and he had lots of cattle—not so much, but enough to butcher at times.

I like to garden. I remember garden peas. The green ones. Not the black-eyed peas. We had a big garden, much too big

* Egg bread is made by adding eggs to the cornmeal and liquid mixture.

for the size of the family. I'd pick a bushel or more, and we didn't need them, so you'd give them to the neighbors who didn't have them. That's the way you *did*. It was no hassle about it. I don't think it ever occurred to our immediate family to indoctrinate children against sharing. Because they had had the privilege of growing up where they'd raised a lot of food. They were never hungry. They could share their food with people. And so, you share your *lives* with people.

Many a night I have gotten up after we moved to North Carolina. I have gotten up in the middle of the night when somebody knocked on the door. The train had brought somebody up who was coming either to a marriage or funeral of a relative. The first thing you asked, you would ask if they wanted to eat something. If necessary, we'd get up and make a fire and heat the coffee, and heat up the food that was left over. Whatever was necessary to make people comfortable. And, it so happened that this is part of what came down as heritage.

That's my maternal grandmother in that picture. She's holding a grandchild. She was about ninety-four or ninety-five then, shortly before she passed. And she's on what is part of the old slave plantation on which she was a slave, and which the family has owned since shortly after Emancipation. She had three daughters. My mother was one. I had an aunt who had no children, then I had an aunt who had thirteen.

My grandmother never would live as such with her children after they were grown. I was in college when she died. But she remained on the old place. And 'cross the road from her place her son had his home. One son stayed home till the grandpa passed. And then she had a daughter who lived at a house nearby. They were close enough for her, if necessary, to call them. And they were close enough, if they wanted, to bring her food. A daughter-in-law wanted to bring her breakfast—she wouldn't have it. She said no. She did her own cooking. If she wanted to go over to have a meal she'd *go*. But she didn't want anybody thinking they had to bring her breakfast every morning or send dinner every day.

When I went to see her the last time, and any time that I went, she'd do her own cooking. And she had moved out of the kitchen into cooking on the hearth in her bedroom. Now why that. The pattern which came out of the period of slavery, of having a kitchen separated from the house, was one that was followed by persons like my grandparents. Kitchens were a little distance from the house. You didn't have all this grease coming in through "the master's house," so they didn't either. But when the children left, she just forgot about the outside kitchen and did her cooking for herself right in her bedroom. She had two beds, and when I'd go visit her I'd sleep in one, the master bed that she and Grandpa'd slept in all along. And I guess she lived—she had to live 'bout thirty years or more after he passed.

My aunt who had thirteen children of her own raised three more. She had become a midwife, and a child was born who was covered with sores. Nobody was particularly wanting the child, so she took the child and raised him. He's one of the *best* of her brood. And another mother decided she didn't want to be bothered with two children. So my aunt took one and raised him. So they were part of the family.

I remember we rented some land after we moved to North Carolina. And the farmer who was living there had lots of children and seemingly nothing else. And his wife died. And so the little ones would be very unkempt, and part of my weekend "pleasures" was to go over with clean clothes and try to catch the young ones and give 'em a bath. Being the nonfearing type, I didn't have to be but so big, I was ten or twelve at the time. So you see, I'd tackle them. Mama would say, "You must take the clothes to Mr. Powell's house, and give so-and-so a bath." The children were running sort of wild, because I guess he began to have other interests. The kids for the devilment would take off across the field. We'd chase them down, and bring them back, and put 'em in the tub, and wash 'em off, and change clothes, and carry the dirty ones home, and wash them. Those kind of things were routine.

Mama was always responding to the sick after we moved. There was a woman and a man who were lacking in mental capacity. But they had an offspring. And one day I was walking to the post office, and Mandy, I think we called her, was standing in her doorway on her little porch, and she was bleeding. I wasn't too aware then of the menstrual period. But I knew this was more blood than anybody *should* be having, just standing. So when I came back home I told mama, and so she went down, and the woman was having, I don't know whether it was a hemorrhage or just *what*. She needed medical attention. So what do you *do*? I mean, she was a *person*. You couldn't just pass by her and say, "Oh, that's just Mandy Bunk, you see, who also raised her pig in one room and herself in the other room." You don't do that. At least this is the way we happened to grow up.

My father took care of people too, but see, my father had to work, poor little devil! See, after we moved to the country, he remained in the city and would come home periodically. My father ran on a boat, as a waiter, from Norfolk to Washington. At one point, that was the only transportation from Norfolk, Virginia, to Washington, D.C. You didn't have bridges. Norfolk, like New York, is almost surrounded by water. And so the major transportation, for commercial reasons and passengers, were these ships. And he was on the passenger ships. Every night he was on the water. One day he was in Washington, and the next day he was in Norfolk. He saw to it that each of us made the trip.

Where we lived there was no sense of hierarchy, in terms of those who have, having a right to look down upon, or to evaluate as a lesser breed, those who didn't have. Part of that could have resulted, I think, from two factors. One was the proximity of my maternal grandparents to slavery. They had known what it was to not have. Plus, my grandfather had gone into the Baptist ministry, and that was part of the quote, unquote, Christian concept of sharing with others. I went to a school that went in for Christian training. Then, there were people who "stood for something," as I call it. Your relationship to human beings was more important than your relationship to the amount of money that you made.

There was a deep sense of community that prevailed in this

little neck of the woods. It wasn't a town, it was just people. And each of them had their twenty-thirty-forty-fifty acre farms, and if there were emergencies, the farmer next to you would share in something to meet that emergency. For instance, when you thresh wheat, if there was a thresher around, you didn't have each person having his own. So you came to my farm and threshed, then you went to the next one and the next one and the next one. You joined in. Part of the land was on a riverbank, the Roanoke River, and now it has been made into a lake through a dam process. But the river would overflow at times and certain crops might be ruined. So if that took place, and it wrecked havoc with the food supply, I am told that my grandfather would take his horse and wagon and go up to the county seat, which was the only town at that point, and mortgage, if necessary, his land, to see that people ate.

The sense of community was pervasive in the black community as a whole, I mean especially the community that had a sense of roots. This community had been composed to a large extent by relatives. Over the hill was my grandfather's sister who was married to my Uncle Carter, and up the grove was another relative who had a place. So it was a deep sense of community. I think these are the things that helped to strengthen my concept about the need for people to have a sense of their own value, and *their* strengths, and it became accentuated when I began to travel in the forties for the National Association for the Advancement of Colored People. Because during that period, in the forties, racial segregation and discrimination were very harsh. As people moved to towns and cities, the sense of community diminished. A given area was made up of people from various and sundry other areas. They didn't come from the same place. So they had to *learn* each other, and they came into patterns of living that they had not been accustomed to. And so whatever deep sense of community that may have been developed in that little place that I spoke of, didn't always carry over to the city when they migrated. They lost their roots. When you lose that, what will you do next. You *hope* that you begin to think in terms of the *wider* brotherhood.

Widening the Community

Hard times is here everywhere you go,
  Times are harder than ever been befo'.
You know that people, they all driftin' from do' to do',
  But they caint find no heaven, I don't care where they go.
People, if I ever can git off this ol' hard killin' flo',
  Lord, I'll never git down this low no mo'.
When you hear me singin' this ol' lonesome song,
  People, you know these hard times caint last us so long.
You know you say you had money, you better be sho',
  Lord, these hard times gon' kill you, jes' drive on slow.

—*Skip James, "Hard Time Killin' Floor Blues."*

The Great Depression struck in 1929. It lasted until World
War II. Big business, overinvested in a frenzied drive to expand,
collapsed. Millions of people lost their jobs. In the Midwest
and Southwest, drought caused blinding dust storms. Like a
shroud, the dust settled over houses, plants, ploughs, animals.
Banks foreclosed mortgages, and millions of people were
evicted from their homes. Counseled to tighten their belts
further, the American people fought back. A radical spirit was
in the air. News of tenant organizing, eviction blockings, rent
strikes, wildcat strikes in factories, and other grassroots action
filled the daily newspapers.

Two years after Ella Baker graduated from Shaw University
in Raleigh, North Carolina, "the crash" hit. She had dreamed
of going to the University of Chicago to learn sociology. But
times were hard:

I came to New York in the summer of 1927. See, I refused to teach. The
reason I refused was primarily because this was the thing that everybody figures you could do. And if you didn't teach, what *did* you do?
This was true as far as blacks were concerned, and particularly black
women. I had my sights on going to the University of Chicago but
you can't go to Chicago and make it as easily with nothing as you
could in New York. I had a cousin who my mother raised who was
working and whose husband was working, so I came, I stayed with
her.[1]

In New York City, Baker found that for all her education, she
could get only waitressing and factory work: she was black.

Other people were out of work altogether. "The tragedy of see-ing long lines of people standing waiting, actually waiting on the bread line, for coffee or handouts, this had its impact," she said. She helped form the Young Negroes' Cooperative League. There, she began organizing consumer cooperatives—group buying. She was hired by the Works Progress Administration to continue her speaking, writing, and teaching about con-sumer affairs. The Works Progress Administration—the WPA, as everyone familiarly called it—was set up under Franklin Delano Roosevelt to help solve the astronomical unemploy-ment of the Depression. It employed thousands of people—construction workers, teachers, writers, artists, musicians, photographers. Roads, schools, and housing were built. Wall murals were painted. Plays and films were written and pro-duced. The consumer education movement Ella Baker de-scribes is little known. Its black participants, especially, have been hidden from history. It is similar in certain respects to the consumer co-ops and the education drives that we know today.

I think it was 1932, we organized the Young Negroes' Coopera-tive League. Basically, we started out from the virtue of buying together, as over against separately. To buy for your group. And therefore save, you see. And there were even cooperative restaurants around, downtown. But they've gone now. George Schuyler now is considered a very reactionary writer, but he was part of the new renaissance of black writers, and he was a columnist on the Pittsburgh *Courier,* which had a wide circula-tion.[2] Among the issues that he raised was the question of con-sumer buying power. Some young people wrote in response to George's column, and we met. The first meeting that we had was in Washington, and then we'd meet in Pittsburgh. I served as the coordinator, sending out the information. It was down on Twelfth Street we had offices.

The Young Negroes' Cooperative League had representation throughout the country. One group over in Philadelphia that started a store also had a little farm out in Doylestown, Pennsyl-vania. And then we had a medical man and his wife up in Buffalo, New York. They spearheaded what was a very good cooperative store for a while. And in the housing development in Chicago, some cooperatives started.

By the time the WPA came, I had done a little writing and a little talking about consumer awareness. In the WPA, we developed a brochure, a little mimeographed thing that raised the question of quality: why you judge the quality of goods; what you buy; where you could buy best; how best you could use your buying power. At that stage, people were more aware of how little they had, so if they could band together and buy a little cheaper, it had an appeal. People were feeling the pinch, so when people feel the pinch they do certain things that they wouldn't do otherwise. And so we had classes in the settlement houses or in women's clubs or wherever else you could.

During this time, I went everywhere there was discussion. New York was not as hazardous as it now is. You could walk the streets at three o'clock in the morning. And so wherever there was a discussion, I'd go. It didn't matter if it was all men. I've been in many groups where there were all men, and maybe I was the only woman, or the only black, it didn't matter. Because I was filling my cup, as it were. I drank of the "nectar divine." I was open to all kinds of discussions. I'd never heard any discussions about the social revolution, because, basically, Shaw University was run by the Northern Baptist Convention, and they were "clas-si-cal-ly" inclined! The English teacher that I had through my college years was Dr. Benjamin Brawley, who came from an educated family in the South, but he got his degree from "Hahvahd"! And he was quite a stickler for not even letting you read all the nice salacious things that were in Shakespeare. He would never let himself be in a classroom after class by himself with one girl!

When I came here, there was a greater participation in the Harlem area than now. You see, New York was the hotbed of— let's call it radical thinking. You had every spectrum of radical thinking on WPA. We had a lovely time! The ignorant ones, like me, we had lots of opportunity to hear and to evaluate whether or not this was the kind of thing you wanted to get into. Boy it was *good*, stimulating!

The NAACP Years

Southern trees bear a strange fruit,
Blood on the leaves and blood at the root,
Black bodies swinging in the Southern breeze,
Strange fruit hanging from the poplar trees.

—*Billie Holiday song.*

The National Association for the Advancement of Colored People was founded in 1910. It was five years after "The Niagara Movement"—a group of young black men, including the great historian and activist W. E. B. DuBois—had first met and resolved dedicatedly to oppose white terrorism and oppression. It was three years after whites in Springfield, Illinois, had invaded the black neighborhood of that city, destroying businesses with guns, axes, and other implements; lynching two black men; and injuring over seventy people. Such terrorism was not new. It had gone on since slavery days. Blacks were cheap labor and good scapegoats. The poorest whites had one thing to be thankful for: at least they weren't black. Whites, who benefited from the way things were, fought against changes in the status quo. There were riots and waves of lynchings. Black men and women were burned alive. Local newspapers routinely reported on these acts of terrorism against black people, as in the following 1904 account from the Vicksburg, Mississippi *Evening Post:*

When the two Negroes were captured they were tied to trees and while the funeral pyres were being prepared they were forced to suffer the most fiendish tortures. The blacks were forced to hold out their hands while one finger at a time was chopped off. The fingers were distributed [to the surrounding white mob] as souvenirs.

The National Association for the Advancement of Colored People was founded to seek police protection for blacks in the North and the South alike; to launch an antilynching crusade; and to begin antisegregation drives through education and legal action. "The Association," Ella Baker said, beginning to

(*text continued on page 68*)

FOR CIVIL RIGHTS

Far right:
Ella Baker
speaking at a
Southern Conference
Educational Fund dinner
in the 1960s. **1**: Blake Baker, father.
2: Georgianna Baker, mother.
3: Ella Baker's grandmother, with
one of her grandchildren.
4: Baker at a Southern Conference
Educational Fund board
meeting, 1966. **5**: Baker as a young
woman. **6**: Baker and Ruby Dee
at Jeanette Rankin News
Conference, 1968. **7**: Baker at
her 75th birthday party,
1978. **8**: In her Harlem
apartment, 1978.

ELLA BAKER

speak of her first days with the NAACP, "had been in existence
since 1910. And over the period of years of its work, the issues
that surfaced, the tragedies that took place like the lynchings
—this became the basis for organizing *people.* Around what
was happening." Ella Baker began working for the NAACP in
the early thirties, and continued through the early fifties. In the
thirties, she traveled for the organization, recruiting members,
particularly in the South. In the early forties, she worked as
assistant field secretary for the NAACP; later, she was made
national director of branches (local chapters). In the fifties, in
New York City, she served as president of that city's branch of
the NAACP. There, she worked on school desegregation:

New York City didn't act right after the '54 decision.* It didn't have
any reason to act, so you had to help it to realize it. I was asked to
serve on the Mayor's Commission. They finally discovered the city
wasn't integrated! And Bob Wagner the second was then mayor, and
we ended up by having several sessions with him. In '57, the entire
summer was spent in weekly parent workshops, helping parents become aware that they had certain rights. I have been in school offices,
and some little parent would walk in, and nobody would pay any
attention to him. Not even ask, "Can I help you?"

Ella Baker's greatest effort as an organizer was to awaken in
her listeners the feeling of common need and a sense that in
numbers there is strength. The black teacher or businessperson
still shared a common history and danger with the black tenant
farmer, laborer, or domestic. But only if the poor overcame
their terror would they join the National Association for the
Advancement of Colored People. And only if the well-to-do
overcame their snobbery, their false sense of security, would
they open their churches to the organization, find offices for
it, and give money to it. It isn't easy to convince people to overcome such feelings. Baker could. People seemed to feel her one
of them, no matter what their status.

* On May 17, 1954, the Supreme Court ruled that segregation of Negro children in public schools was unconstitutional. The ruling was one thing—
implementing it was another. It took a decade of civil rights struggles to bring
to light the massive resistance of both southern and northern whites to school
integration. And that resistance continues, as busing battles in Boston and
other cities in the 1970s show.

Ella Baker began her work for the NAACP as a field organizer, someone who travels to different cities, towns, and rural
areas trying to recruit new people to an organization and raise
money. How does a field organizer begin? When you go to a
place you don't know, how do you find people who will introduce you into the community? How do you help the fearful
overcome their fear and sign up for work? How do you persuade
the well-off that they have a kinship with the poor? Out of such
questions, the following reminiscences flow.

The first aspect of being on the field staff was to help. You
helped raise money. You conducted membership campaigns in
different areas. A new person coming on the field would learn
how to campaign, and then you would be sent to smaller terri-
tory. I started in Florida. I'd never been there before.

The NAACP had a roster of people who were in contact, who
were members. And so when you go out in the field, if they had
a branch, say, in Sanford or Clearwater, Florida, you had been in
correspondence there. So you make your contact with the person in Tampa who's said to the community, "Miss so-and-so's
coming in." And so you go down, and they have provided some
space in somebody's church or office or somewhere you had
access to a telephone.

Where did people gather? They gathered in churches. In
schools. And you'd get permission. You'd call up Reverend
Brother so-and-so, and ask if you could appear before the congregation at such-and-such a time. Sometimes they'd give you
three minutes, because, after all, many people weren't secure
enough to run the risk, as they saw it, of being targeted as ready
to challenge the powers that be. And they'd say, "You have
three minutes after the church service." And you'd take it. And
you'd use it, to the extent to which you can be persuasive. It's
the ammunition you have. That's all you have.

We dealt with what was most pressing for a given section.
For instance, Harry T. Moore was one of three black principals
in Florida who was fired when they began to talk in terms of
equal pay. The differential between black and white teachers
was tragic, to say the least. Many times, money had been
"appropriated" for black education and it had been diverted to

other sources. And, of course, there wasn't headlines on that, they just didn't *get* there, see.

Harry T. Moore's house was bombed from under him one night. And he was killed as a result. This particular night, I think it was Christmas eve, '46, dynamite was placed under his bedroom. He and his wife were blown to smithereens. There were a lot of people whom Harry T. Moore had benefited. We talked to them. He helped them get their pay when they had worked and didn't get paid. So you could go into that area of Florida and you could talk about the virtue of NAACP, because they knew Harry T. Moore. They hadn't discussed a whole lot of theory. But there was a *man* who served *their* interests and who *identified* with them.

On what basis do you seek to organize people? Do you start to try to organize them on the fact of what *you* think, or what they are first interested in? You start where the *people* are. Identification with people. There's always this problem in the minority group that's escalating up the ladder in this culture, I think. Those who have gotten some training and those who have gotten some material gains, it's always the problem of their not understanding the possibility of being divorced from those who are not in their social classification. Now, there were those who felt they had made it, would be embarrassed by the fact that some people would get drunk and get in jail, and so they wouldn't be concerned too much about whether they were brutalized in jail. 'Cause he was a *drunk!* He was a so-and-so. Or she was a streetwalker. We get caught in that bag. And so you have to help break that down without alienating them at the same time. The gal who has been able to buy her minks and whose husband is a professional, they live well. You can't insult her, you never go and tell her she's a so-and-so for taking, for *not* identifying. You try to point out where her interest lies in identifying with that other one across the tracks who doesn't have minks.

How do you do that? You don't always succeed, but you try. You'd point out what had happened, in certain cases, where whole communities were almost destroyed by police brutality on a large scale. They went and burned down the better homes. In Tampa, Florida, I met some of those people whose homes were burned down. These were people I'd call middle class. The men got the guns, and they carried their womenfolk and the children into the woods. And they stood guard. Some stood guard over the people in the woods, and they stood guard over their homes and property, ready to shoot. So what you do is to cite examples that had taken place somewhere else. You had to be persuasive on the basis of fact. You cite it, you see. This can happen to *you*. Sometimes you're able to cite instances of where there's been a little epidemic, or an outbreak of the more devastating kinds of disease. You point out that those of us who live across the railroad track and are in greater filth or lack of sanitation can have an effect on you who live on the other side, 'cause disease doesn't have such a long barrier between us, you see. As long as the violations of the rights of Tom Jones could take place with impunity, you are not secure. So you helped to reestablish a sense of identity of each with the struggle.

Of course, your success depended on both your disposition and your capacity to sort of stimulate people—and how you carried yourself, in terms of not being above people. And see, there were more people who were not economically secure than there were economically secure people. I didn't *have* any mink—I don't have any now—but you don't go into a group where minks are prohibitive in terms of getting them and carry your minks and throw 'em around. Why, they can't get past *that*. They can't get past the fact that you got minks and they don't have mink. And see, I had no problems 'cause I didn't have none. Nor did I have aspirations for these things.

I remember one place I got a contribution for a life membership in the NAACP, which was five-hundred dollars then, was from a longshoremen's union. They remembered somebody who had been there before from the NAACP, with a mink coat. When they gave this five-hundred dollar membership, somebody mentioned it. See, they had resented the mink coat. I don't think it was the mink coat that they really resented. It was the *barrier* they could sense between them and the person in the coat. See, you can have a mink coat on and you can identify with the man who is working on the docks. If you got it, if you *really* identify with him, what you wear won't make a damn bit of difference. But if you talk differently, and somehow talk down to people, they can sense it. They can feel it. And they know whether you are talking *with* them, or talking *at* them, or talking *about* them.

If you feel that you are part of them and they are part of you, you don't *say* "I'm-a-part-of-you." What you really do is, you point out something. Especially the lower-class people, the people who'd felt the heel of oppression, see, they *knew* what you were talking about when you spoke about police brutality. They *knew* what you were speaking about when you talked about working at a job, doing the same work, and getting a differential in pay. And if your sense of being a part of them got over to them, they appreciated that. Somebody would get the point. Somebody would come out and say, "I'm gon' join that darn organization." As an example, I remember in someplace out of St. Petersburg, Florida, the first time I'd ever been to the Holy and Sanctified church. We had a good response. One lady came out and all she could say was how my dress was the same as hers. Now, she didn't know how to deal with issues. But she identified. And she joined.

And, then you have to recognize what people *can* do. There're some people in my experience, especially "the little people" as some might call them, who never could explain the NAACP as such. But they had the knack of getting money from John Jones or somebody. They might walk up to him: "Gimme a dollar for the NAACP." And maybe because of what they had done in relationship to John Jones, he'd give the dollar. They could never tell anybody what the program of the Association was. So what do you do about that. You don't be demeaning them. You say, well here is Mrs. Jones, Mrs. Susie Jones, and remember last year Sister Susie Jones came in with so much. And Sister Susie Jones would go on *next* year and get this money. Now, somewhere in the process she may learn some other methods, and she may learn to articulate some of the program of the Association. But whether she does or not, she *feels* it. And she transmits it to those she can talk to. And she might end up just saying, "You ain't doin' nothin' but spendin' your money down at that so-and-so place." She may shame him. Or she may say, "Boy, I know your mama." And so you start talkin' about what the mothers would like for them to do. So you do it because there's mama, mama's callin'. See, somewhere down the line this becomes important to them. At least these are the ways I saw it. And I think they respond.

Daily Fundamentals

How did I make my living? I haven't. I have eked out existence.

—Ella Baker.

We asked Ella Baker how she had earned her living. We also asked about childrearing. She told us, "I didn't have any children, I didn't beget any. I wasn't interested, really, in having children *per se*. I didn't have all the advantages young ladies have now, protecting themselves from pregnancy. But it just didn't happen." We asked her how long she had had her niece, and she replied, laughing, "Through college. She's still living, she's raising me now."

In school, I waited tables and had charge of a chemistry laboratory, and that provided a certain amount of money to help pay tuition, because my parents had three children in boarding school at the same time and no real money. The summer after school, I worked in a hotel—we called it "a roadhouse." A rich lady had this place, and she decided I was to be the one to wait on her table.

'Course we organized the group that was working out there that summer. We started out with a guy named Uncle Charlie. I don't know what his nationality was—we were all mixed up in nationality—but he had the entertainment. There was a girl who had a very beautiful voice, and I usually would announce things. But if something came up that I didn't like, I'd react to it. I retained what I called my essential integrity. I neither kowtowed nor felt it necessary to lord it over anyone else. If I were, let's call it the head waitress, I didn't find it necessary to lord it over the man who washed dishes in the kitchen. Somewhere down the line I had a deep sense of my being part of humanity, and this I've always tried to preserve.

At various times, I worked for newspapers. I used to send in some stories to the black newspapers, and sometimes I'd get paid. I worked with a couple of newspapers of short vintage which were black-based, an American West Indian newspaper I think was the first one here in New York. When George Schuyler organized the *Negro National News*, I was the office manager there. A lot of the young black columnists you see now in the black press were youngsters then, and they came through there.

Then I was with the WPA workers' education, the consumer education project. I got top salary. I was a teacher and teachers were paid more than some of the others. Then the NAACP paid me. At first, all of two thousand dollars a year, which maybe at that stage people could live on.

I had to resign from the NAACP in 1946 because I had taken on the responsibility of raising a niece, and I knew I could not travel as widely when I took her.[3] She was about seven or eight then.

I think today, people's concept of political organizing is like you're really out there night and day doing it all. See, young people today have had the luxury of a period in which they could give their all to this political organizing. They didn't have to be bothered by a whole lot of other things. But most of those who are older put it in with the things that they had to do.

The Beginnings of the Movement

*He pulled up the top and reached for a bottle. "That'll be a nickel,"
he said. "You drink it here."*

*"But ... but ... I don't want a Coke from the bottle. I want to sit
up there and drink my Coke from a glass. Why do I have to drink
it here?" The man looked at me. Something was wrong. I didn't know
what, but something. A fear swelled within me, the fear of the
unknown. ...*

*"You have to drink your Coke back here. You can't sit on these
stools."*

But . . . why!" By this time I had the cold Coca-Cola in my hands.
It was very wet and very cold and I felt myself turning cold like the
bottle of Coke. Something dreadful was wrong and I could not
understand why I was crying, what was the matter, who this man
was, what right he had to tell me where I had to drink my Coke, why
I couldn't sit on the stool. . . .

"Well, don't you know!"

"Know what!"

"Boy, you're a nigger," he said in a flat voice.

"A what!" I asked. I heard him and I didn't hear him because I
didn't really understand the word.

"A nigger, and Negroes don't sit on the stools here."

—*James Forman, description of a childhood experience in the 1940s,*
The Making of Black Revolutionaries *(1972).*

Black resistance to oppression began in the ships that brought
West Africans to America to be slaves. There were small, personal acts—the handing down of language, tradition, and
memories among friends, and from parents to children. There
were large, public acts, like mutinies on slave ships. From
slavery days through the 1940s, where the previous part of Ella
Baker's story left off, black women and men took individual
and group stands against government, masters, and employers.
They sang their sorrow and asserted the facts of their lives in
the blues. They established organizations, like the National
Association for the Advancement of Colored People, for legal
and political action.

There have been times when the grassroots movement has
been more visible than others, and periods when it has seemed
to disappear altogether. Such a time of "disappearance" was the
decade between the mid-forties and fifties. There were no
visible signs of life—few group protests or mass demonstrations. There was a cold war on, not only against communism
but against the idea that ordinary people might change the
course of history.

But even during a time like the cold war, people were still
active and kept ideals and commitment alive. Take a man
named Amzie Moore, long-time friend and NAACP associate of
Ella Baker, who returned from the segregated Armed Forces of

World War II to the heart of Mississippi—a terror state for southern blacks. There, he initiated a drive, one of the first since the 1870s, to register black people to vote. Amzie Moore and others like him are not in history books even now. But they made contact with people around them. And when the black students of the late fifties and early sixties decided to take action in the South, it was to people like Amzie Moore and the black dentist Ella Baker mentions below, that they went for advice.

The shockwave that caused a visible crack in the cold war glacier began in 1955. In Montgomery, Alabama, a black woman named Rosa Parks refused to yield her bus seat to a white passenger. Parks, secretary of the Alabama NAACP, was arrested. Like lunch counters, drinking fountains, swimming pools, toilets, and other public facilities, buses had been segregated in the South by custom since slavery. They had been segregated by law since 1896, when the Supreme Court, in a decision that would set back black civil rights for sixty years, declared "the enforced separation of the two races" the law of the land.[4] On Rosa Parks's arrest, Montgomery's black citizens started a 381-day boycott of the city's buses. For over a year, they walked. As they were the city's main users of the bus system, they brought public transportation to a halt.

The Southern Christian Leadership Conference was founded in 1957 by Martin Luther King and other ministers, on the heels of the Montgomery bus boycott. The founders of SCLC knew that if a mass movement is to grow from a single gesture of protest, people must *keep on* acting and demonstrating. The organization's original idea of how to keep the movement going was a crusade for citizenship—voter registration. But voter registration did not become a reality until some five years later. And then, it did not come by way of SCLC, but from a very different group, the Student Nonviolent Coordinating Committee.

Instead, sit-ins became the main actions of the movement, beginning in 1960, when four freshmen from A & T College in Greensboro, North Carolina, sat down at a Woolworth's lunch counter to challenge segregation. The sit-ins spread in waves across the South, involving thousands of black students and some whites. The philosophy behind the sit-ins was "nonviolent direct action."[5] The decision to take direct action—to sit in, demonstrate, picket segregated facilities—sprang from the realization that it would take more than going through the orderly channels of government to combat racism. As direct action protests were met with violence by police and white hoodlums and mobs, the evidence of racism was displayed graphically on front pages of newspapers and on television screens.

When SNCC was founded, the members of the Student Nonviolent Coordinating Committee believed that their actions must always be taken in a spirit of love and forgiveness. "Love," asserted the SNCC credo adopted in April 1960, "is the central motif of nonviolence. . . . Such love goes to the extreme; it remains loving and forgiving even in the midst of hostility. It matches the capacity of evil to inflict suffering with an even more enduring capacity to absorb evil, all the while persisting in love." Translated in deeds, the philosophy meant that if police came to arrest you, you did not resist, you simply went limp. If, at a demonstration or elsewhere, someone attacked you, you fell to the ground, protecting your most vulnerable parts by drawing your knees up to your chest, and protecting your head by cupping your hands over it.

To remain nonviolent in the face of violence required a great deal of training and discipline. "Nonviolent direct action" was a Christian idea, Ella Baker explains. "For a long time the church had been the center of whatever activity or leadership for change there was in the black community. I think the reason they were able to be so disciplined, the earlier sit-inners, was because they were for the most part church-oriented."

From 1960 to 1965, many black and white civil rights activists and black citizens were teargassed, clubbed, shot, poked with electrically-charged cattle prods, and tortured in jail. Some people were brutally murdered, including three young student activists, Michael Schwerner, James Chaney, and

(text continued on page 82)

Making History

Ella Baker's political organizing work began during the Depression and continues into the present. Baker was one of the most influential organizers of the black civil rights movement of the 1960s.
1: Breadline of unemployed people, Brooklyn, New York, 1935.
2: Voter registration, Clinton, Alabama, 1964.
3: Arrests being made during picketing of an Atlanta induction center, 1967.
4: Citizens Cooperative Society Store, Buffalo, New York, 1930s.
5: Mississippi Freedom Democratic Party, Madison County convention, 1964. **6:** Civil rights demonstrator.
7: Ella Baker and Fannie Lou Hamer, Mississippi Freedom Democratic Party, 1964. **8:** Third World Women's Coordinating Committee; Ella Baker, third from left.

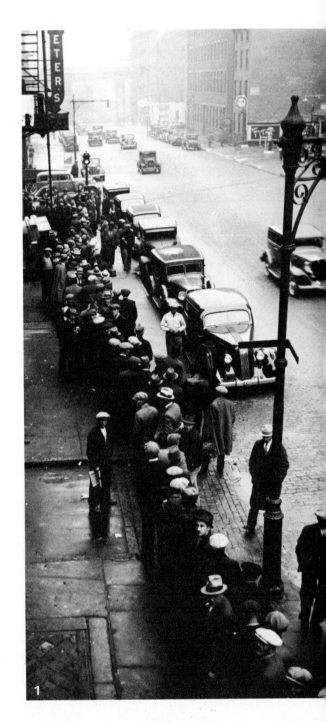

81

Andrew Goodman. On a quiet Sunday morning in Birmingham, Alabama, in 1963, whites bombed a church. Four young black girls, aged eleven to fourteen, were killed.

Many—Ella Baker was one—recoiled at the thought of not defending themselves when attacked.

I frankly could not have sat and let someone put a burning cigarette on the back of my neck as some young people did. Whether this is right or wrong or good or bad, I have already been conditioned, and I have not seen anything in the nonviolent technique that can dissuade me from challenging somebody who wants to step on my neck. If necessary, if they hit me, I might hit them back.

In fact, a turning point in the civil rights movement came in the mid-sixties as the notion of a more militant "black power" movement superseded the early movement of nonviolent civil disobedience. But that movement of nonviolent direct action shook the nation to its foundations in the early sixties. And the idea of revolution—a radical change in the way a nation is governed, a faith in the power of the oppressed majority to change the way things are done in a country—was reborn in the United States in this stubborn, daring, Christian wave of sit-ins. We asked Ella Baker: Had the sit-ins seemed revolutionary to her? How had they come to be?

I guess revolutionary is relative to the situations that people find themselves in, and whatever their goals are, and how many people are in agreement that this is a desired goal. The original four kids who sat down in Greensboro, North Carolina, I'm confident that they had little or no knowledge of the revolutionary background that people talk about when they speak of changing the society by way of socialism or communism. They were youngsters who had a very simple reaction to an inequity. When you're a student with no money, and you go buy what you need like your paper or your pencils, where do you go? The five-and-ten-cent-store. At least you could then, because the prices were not quite as disproportionate as they are now. These two had been talking with a dentist, a black dentist who apparently had some experience with the earlier days of the formation of the

Congress of Racial Equality (CORE). They were able to talk with him about their frustrations, going in there, spending all their little money, and yet not being able to sit and buy a five-cent Coke. That was a rather simple challenge as you look back. They decided they were going to do something about it, and so they sat down. Then some others followed their actions. A sister who had a brother in school in another town, her town had already sat in. She might call and ask, why doesn't his school sit in? This was the communication link, plus the media. They sat, and the others came and sat, and it spread. I guess one of the reasons it spread was because it was simple, and it struck home to a lot of young people who were in school.

It hadn't gone on so long before I suggested that we call a conference of the sit-inners to be held in Raleigh. It was very obvious to the Southern Christian Leadership Conference that there was little or no communication between those who sat in, say, in Charlotte, North Carolina, and those who eventually sat in at some other place in Virginia or Alabama. They were motivated by what the North Carolina four had started, but they were not in contact with each other, which meant that you couldn't build a sustaining force just based on spontaneity.

My estimate was that the conference would bring together a couple hundred of the young leadership. I had not hoped for such large numbers of adults who came. These adults were part and parcel of groups such as the Montgomery bus boycott. They also may have been relating to the organizing first steps of SCLC, which had been officially established but had not expanded very much.

We ended up with about three hundred people. We had insisted that the young people be left to make their own decisions. Also, we provided for those who came from outside the South to meet separately from those who came from the sit-in areas, because the persons who came from, say, New York, frequently had had wider experience in organizing and were too articulate. In the initial portion of the conference, the southern students had the right to meet, to discuss, and to determine where they wanted to go. It wasn't my idea to separate the northern and southern students. I hesitated to project ideas as pointedly as that, but those who had worked closely with me knew that I believed very firmly in the right of the people who were under the heel to be the ones to decide what action they were going to take to get from under their oppression. As a group, basically, they were the black students from the South. The heritage of the South was theirs, and it was one of oppression. Those who came from the other nineteen schools and colleges and universities up North didn't have the same oppression, and they were white. They were much more erudite and articulate, farther advanced in the theoretical concepts of social change. This can become overwhelming for those who don't even understand what you're talking about and feel put down.

The Southern Christian Leadership Conference felt that they could influence how things went. They were interested in having the students become an arm of SCLC. They were most confident that this would be their baby, because I was their functionary and I had called the meeting. At a discussion called by the Reverend Dr. King, the SCLC leadership made decisions who would speak to whom to influence the students to become part of SCLC. Well, I disagreed. There was no student at Dr. King's meeting. I was the nearest thing to a student, being the advocate, you see. I also knew from the beginning that having a woman be an executive of SCLC was not something that would go over with the male-dominated leadership. And then, of course, my personality wasn't right, in the sense I was not afraid to disagree with the higher authorities. I wasn't one to say, yes, because it came from the Reverend King. So when it was proposed that the leadership could influence the direction by speaking to, let's say, the man from Virginia, he could speak to the leadership of the Virginia student group, and the assumption was that having spoken to so-and-so, so-and-so would do what they wanted done, I was outraged. I walked out.

SNCC and Voter Registration

The issue is power. We control the state and we're not going to allow any Negras to run Alabama and take our power from us. . . . If we allow the Negras to crack our power in any way, this is an

*invitation to further weaken it. Why, in the county where my friend
lives, the Negras are nine to one and his father is sheriff of that
county. Do you think if the Negras had the right to vote that they
would elect his father as sheriff? We got the power and we intend to
keep it.*

—*Statement by John Patterson, son of the then governor of Alabama,
at the 1956 national meeting of the National Student Association,
quoted by James Forman,* The Making of Black Revolutionaries
(1972).

Ella Baker left the Southern Christian Leadership Conference in
August 1960, and went to work for the Student Nonviolent
Coordinating Committee. She earned money working part-
time for the YWCA in Atlanta. But she spent most of her days
staffing the tiny SNCC office—which she had found space for
through black businessmen friendly to the cause—on Auburn
Avenue in Atlanta, Georgia. She worked there with two young
people, Jane Stembridge, a white student from Georgia, who
was studying theology in New York City, and Bob Moses, a
black teacher in his mid-twenties from New York.

The Student Nonviolent Coordinating Committee started by
coordinating and continuing the sit-ins. In 1961, "freedom
rides" began, to test rulings by the Supreme Court and the
Interstate Commerce Commission that transportation between
states could not be segregated. In May of 1961, the Congress of
Racial Equality united with SNCC to have black and white
activists ride a bus together from Washington to New Orleans.
The bus ride was catastrophic. In Anniston, Alabama, on
Mother's Day, the bus was surrounded by a white mob and fire-
bombed. It burned to a shell, and several riders were hospital-
ized. Further south, in Birmingham, the riders were surrounded
by a mob of men brandishing iron bars. The men attacked,
chased, and beat several riders bloody and unconscious. Nevertheless, SNCC continued coordinating freedom rides, and the
riders used nonviolent resistance in the face of ceaseless brutality and jailings.

The most important step SNCC took during its first year of
existence was to make voter registration its main activity. Ex-

cept for the early 1870s, when blacks had momentarily gained the vote and even elected some local officials and congressmen, black voting in the South had been stifled.

Trying to register people to vote might seem today an obvious way to combat discrimination. But the proposal touched off furious debate in the Student Nonviolent Coordinating Committee. On one side of the argument were the supporters of voter registration. On the other side were people who feared that in only registering people to vote, SNCC would lose the spiritual fervor of nonviolent direct action. By comparison with the direct confrontations with white mobs and police, voter registration seemed a narrow, legalistic activity. Those who argued for the voting drive said that denial of the opportunity to vote was so blatantly unjust that the registration campaign was absolutely necessary. And in the campaign, they said, there would still be plenty of opportunity for nonviolent direct action.

The structure of SNCC finally got hammered out by having long meetings that would last from six in the evening through early morning, or maybe all day. The first time I ever remember having a charley horse in my leg was after thirty hours that I had been more or less sitting in the same sort of cramped position. Because I felt if we had a table, that the first priority would be for the young people to sit there. I had no ambition to be in the leadership. I was only interested in seeing that a leadership had the chance to develop.

The worst conference I remember was at Highlander Folk School. The issue that surfaced was a debate between the group that believed in nonviolence against the group that wanted to introduce political action, get people registered to vote. The nonviolent faction was adamant against political action. My feeling was that you would have to deal with the political action because of the denials that had obtained. See, people had not been free all along to be political, and there was a concerted action on the part of the powers that be to prevent blacks from participating in politics or even having the chance to register and vote.

When those who advocated going into voter registration

spoke, those who were more highly indoctrinated in the nonviolent approach objected that they didn't want just to go into voter registration. They broke up into a kind of fight—a pulling apart. I never intervened between the struggles if I could avoid it. Most of the youngsters had been trained to believe in or to follow adults if they could. I felt they ought to have a chance to learn to think things through and to make the decisions. But this was a point at which I did have something to say. I hope I helped point out that the people who they were most concerned about lived in areas where they had no political influence; they could not exercise their political right to register and vote without intimidation. This in itself was a justification for whatever political action was being proposed. If they went into these deeply prejudiced areas and started voter registration, they would have an opportunity to exercise nonviolent resistance. It worked out that they began to see that those who went in for voter registration would be challenged so that they would have to endure violence—and resort to the nonviolent concept. So they began to talk in terms of this, and that's how they got into a voter registration program.

Bob Moses started a program of voter registration in McComb, Mississippi, and one of the young men was pistol-whipped, I believe. And then, one of the young high school students who had demonstrated, Brenda Travis, was put into reform school, and things developed from there. And they began to see that they wouldn't have to abandon their nonviolence. In fact, they would be hard put to keep it up.

The National Association for the Advancement of Colored People had not developed to the point of sending out people to the hinterlands to actually have voter registration and leadership clinics and to test the barriers. It was the SNCC people who tested them. An NAACP president, in one particular NAACP town, wanted somebody to come down and hold registration clinics— helping people know what they had to do to qualify, what kind of questions they would be asked, and what kind of difficulties they would encounter. Out of that setting the first of the persons was sort of indoctrinated to go and register and buck the system in those deep places. A couple of other SNCC people

went down, and one of them got shot. That was the beginning
of the Mississippi thrust, the real Mississippi thrust.

The Mississippi Thrust

Gulfport, July 8

*There is no such thing as a completed job until everyone is registered.
When you cheat and take a lunch hour . . . you suddenly find
yourself reviewing a failure or a success to discover the whys:
maybe I should have bullied him slightly, or maybe I should have
talked less—and relied on silences. Did I rush him? Should I never
have mentioned registering at all, and just tried to make friends and
set him at ease? It goes on and on.*

*—From a letter by a northern student registering voters during
Mississippi Summer, 1964.*

One of the high points of the voting campaign was Mississippi
Summer. It was organized by Bob Moses and the Council of
Federated Organizations (COFO), which was made up of the
Student Nonviolent Coordinating Committee, the Southern
Christian Leadership Conference, the Congress of Racial Equality, and the National Association for the Advancement of
Colored People. Northern students were asked to go South to
help in the voter registration activities. Mississippi Summer
was part of the revival of radical spirit among young whites in
America. Many white students went down to Mississippi that
summer. None remained unchanged by the experience. Many
became active shortly thereafter in the movement against the
war in Vietnam and in the women's liberation movement.

After Mississippi Summer, the Student Nonviolent Coordinating Committee decided to organize a separate political party
in Mississippi—the Mississippi Freedom Democratic Party
(MFDP). The MFDP was set up in 1964 as an alternative for
blacks to the regular Democratic party. In most regular party
districts, blacks were prevented from voting. Some whites as
well as blacks voted for the MFDP, which sent its delegates to
the Democratic convention of that year in Atlantic City.

Though these delegates had proof that they had received more votes than the regular Democratic party delegates, the party refused to seat them as Mississippi delegates.[6]

My basic role was, I insisted on being available when SNCC was having crisis meetings. Where they were going, I had been. In terms of going to Mississippi, in terms of trying to reach leadership people in certain areas, most of them I knew. The students would come to me and ask me, if you're going to Mississippi, what? Or who? I had worked with the National Association for the Advancement of Colored People, I had worked with the Southern Christian Leadership Conference, I knew people in all of the sections of the South. When Bob Moses went to Mississippi, I sent him to Amzie Moore, who had been one of the earlier pioneers and had suffered reprisals from his voter registration effort. I had helped to raise money here in New York City for Amzie Moore. I had gone down there and stayed with them and helped with meetings, so I knew the person. I knew he knew the state, and so Bob Moses was able to have an entrée. Here was a man who had never been to Mississippi, and he had somewhere to sleep, to eat, and he had somebody who knew something that could be useful.

Then maybe it was a question of helping to write and talk over certain things—what should be the approach? What should we do? I also went around to the campuses that had Ys. I would deal inevitably with the question, what is SNCC doing? Who are the students who had done these things? Because it tends to follow, that when you're young, especially if you see somebody out there doing something, challenging a system that you say you are concerned about, it makes you a little uneasy, or at least maybe inspires you.

Why '64? Why that summer? The Student Nonviolent Coordinating Committee debated it very pointedly, and they came to the conclusion that it was a necessary political move to invite white students to participate in the program. They were very aware that when a black person got brutalized for attempting to register to vote, this was nothing new, it had been done before. But when the son of a governor or the daughter of a congressman or the daughter and son of people up North who could give money and who had some political clout got involved, it was a challenge to the powers that be.

As for the Mississippi Freedom Democratic Party, my thinking was along these lines. The people who were black in Mississippi, if they were going to organize and have any clout at that stage of the game in the Democratic setup, should have the opportunity to organize themselves to do what they thought they ought to do. And if they wanted to become a Mississippi Freedom Democratic Party, then it was my role to help support that.

I was asked to keynote the Mississippi Freedom Democratic Party's convention in Jackson, preparatory to their going to the Democratic convention in Atlantic City. I also was sent to Washington, where the MFDP decided to set up an office which had in it people who were going out to the hinterlands, carrying the challenge to the Democratic delegates who were going to the convention. They were able to secure commitments from the delegates to support the MFDP's challenge to be seated. President Johnson, of course, was the only person who controlled the '64 convention. He had it in his complete control, and he did not permit anything to come up on the floor, which meant that nothing really did surface.

The MFDP delegates carried up all these files which showed that thousands of people had evidenced their interest in registering to vote by going to beauty parlors and barber shops, churches, or wherever else they could set up a registration booth. This was to counter the prevailing concept that Negroes weren't interested in registering. Great fruit came of it in terms of arousing the people and getting them involved, like Mrs. Johnson of Greenwood and like Mrs. Hamer. There's a woman that had been a timekeeper on a plantation for sixteen or more years, and when she attempted to register to vote she lost her job, her husband lost his, and then she was badly beaten.*

* While Ella Baker is a behind-the-scenes figure, Fannie Lou Hamer was a public orator. She was the keynote speaker for the MFDP at Atlantic City in 1964. In 1977, she died of cancer, after having worked in a cooperative farm movement among blacks in Sunflower County, Mississippi.

Somebody Carries On

It's not hard to interpret what our parents mean by a better world. You know, go to school, son, and get a good education. And what do you do with this? You get a degree, you move out into some little community housing project, you get married, five kids and two cars, and you don't care what's happening. . . . So I think when we talk about growing up in a better world, a new world, we mean changing the world to a different place.

—Cordell Reagan, a nineteen-year-old Student Nonviolent Coordinating Committee activist, in the early 1960s.

Although the Mississippi Freedom Democratic Party did not get its delegates seated at the national convention, many local MFDP leaders were elected to office in Mississippi, and MFDP efforts resulted in the 1967 election of the first black state legislator since Reconstruction, Robert Clark. Founders and members of the Mississippi Freedom Democratic Party, like Ella Baker, have kept on, persistent in their efforts to make a better world. For a number of years, Ella Baker was on the staff of the Southern Conference Educational Fund (SCEF), an organization formed to encourage black and white people to work together in the South, and led for many years by Carl and Anne Braden. Ella Baker remains active in New York City, where she is an adviser to many liberation and human rights groups. She also speaks publicly. She has been particularly active in groups supporting freedom struggles in Zimbabwe (Rhodesia) and South Africa. We asked her: What happened to others in the civil rights movement? And how do you keep going?

I think a number of things happened. The people endured with more sense about what they were involved in. They at least survived with knowledge, and out of it has come various kinds of— let's call it adequate leadership. People are more easily alerted to whether they are getting unusual oppression, and they'll do something. They're quicker to respond now. They would be much less willing to settle for what they had endured before, and they would be more likely to actually go to the Nth degree in revolt, if the pressure of the past were reinstated.

You see, today, they are living in what we call a normal society. The same kinds of denials that we have up here in the
North, to one degree or another they have down there. But the
major pressures, the things that they consider the most oppressive, are lifted. I mean, you don't ride Jim Crow.* You can
even go as far as boycotting the stores, which has gotten the
NAACP in deep water. But the people have taken action. They
can elect the people they want to elect whether they turn out
to be good or not. And they can make the usual mistake of feeling that you can trust those in power, because they have given
you a little power. Whether that's good or bad, I'm not in a
position at this stage to talk too pointedly about. It's no worse
than it is anywhere else. You see, I have grave reservations
about what can be accomplished, anyway, by established political parties.

Maybe there will be a new revolution. I don't think there's
going to be one anytime soon, to be honest—I mean among
blacks nor whites in this country. The best country in the world,
you hear them say. I guess it may be, I haven't lived anywhere
else. But it's not good enough as far as I'm concerned. But I'm
not good enough for the task.

I keep going because I don't see the productive value of being
bitter. What else *do* you do? Do you get so bitter that you give
up, and when young people come and want to talk to me, to
hear about the past and learn from it, am I to say, "Oh, forget it,
go on about your business, I'm bitter." You *can* just say, the
heck with it. I'll break off and do what I need to do. Those of us
who have responsibilities of children and family, somebody's
got to provide some food for them, so you might decide to
concentrate on getting that. I can stand that. But if people
begin to place their values in terms of how high they get in the
political world, or how much worldly goods they accumulate,
or what kind of cars they have, or how much they have in the
bank, that's where I begin to lose respect.

* Jim Crow is a term for segregation laws. It comes from the name of a
character who scraped and shuffled in minstrel (song and dance) shows in pre-
Civil War days.

To me, I'm part of the human family. What the human family will accomplish, I can't control. But it isn't impossible that what those who came along with me went through, might stimulate others to continue to fight for a society that does not have those kinds of problems. Somewhere down the line the numbers increase, the tribe increases. So how do you keep on? I can't help it. I don't claim to have any corner on an answer, but I believe that the struggle is eternal. Somebody else carries on.

THREE:
Jessie Lopez De La Cruz

The Battle for Farmworkers' Rights

By Ellen Cantarow

COMING NORTH IN CALIFORNIA from the mountains around Los Angeles, you enter the San Joaquin (pronounced Wa–keen) Valley a little below a city called Bakersfield. It is flat all around. In the winter, the landscape is colored shades of gray and tan with soft, emerald stretches here and there—alfalfa, grown through irrigation, as are all the Valley's crops. Large wheels of bramble—tumbleweed—rest along the roadsides, reminding you that this valley would be desert if it weren't for the aqueducts and canals that bring the water in.

With irrigation, the San Joaquin Valley is some of the richest farmland in the world, producing more food and fiber than forty-one states in this country put together. It is owned by big

CHRONOLOGY

1919: Jessie Lopez born to Guadalupe Lopez and Bermin Fuentez.

1919–28: Family lives in maternal grandparents house in Anaheim, California, where grandfather works in a cement factory until he has an accident and is fired. Father leaves; Jessie is given her mother's maiden name.

1929–30: Sister, mother, and grandfather die, leaving grandmother, Rita Aguirre de Lopez, to raise her own six children, ages six to twenty-two, and three grandchildren. Family moves to Watts and begins a life of migrant farm work.

1933: Family moves permanently to San Joaquin Valley, living in labor camps and working the crops.

1938: Jessie Lopez marries Arnold De La Cruz in Firebaugh, Ca.

1939–47: The De La Cruzes have six children: Ramon, 1939; Arnold, 1942; Guadalupe, 1943, who dies as an infant; Alfred, 1944; Robert, 1946; Virginia, 1947. Jessie De La Cruz continues working in the fields, with a few months off for each birth.

1956: The De La Cruzes adopt a niece, Susan.

1962: Cesar Chavez visits the De La Cruzes and recruits them to the farmworkers union. Jessie begins organizing for the union on a volunteer basis.

1967: Becomes an official union organizer.

1968–70: Appointed to the Fresno County Economic Opportunity Commission. Teaches English to Mexican Americans. Runs union hiring hall in Parlier.

1972: Is a delegate to the Democratic party national convention. The De La Cruzes and three other families borrow money to buy forty acres of farm land outside Fresno.

1974: Helps found National Land for People.

1977: Attends Farmworkers Free University. Receives award from the League of Mexican American Women for "her outstanding contribution to the farm labor movement."

1977–present: Continues, with her husband and other farmworker families, to harvest bumper crops at cooperative ranch. Goes on speaking tours, talking about family farming, cooperative land ownership, and farmworkers' struggles.

growers and giant corporations, like Southern Pacific Railroad, Standard Oil of California, Bangor Punta (manufacturer of Smith & Wesson Rifles and MACE). But the acres and acres of crops that stretch as far as the eye can see, unbroken by any houses, are grown and harvested by workers, many of whom are Mexican Americans.

Ever since the Spanish invaded the land of Native Americans in the sixteenth century, exploiters of the land, from the Spanish through the giant conglomerates of the twentieth century, have reaped profits through the toil, sweat, and blood of the people who labored. Native Americans were the first to work the land. As the growers' business expanded, they needed large numbers of cheap workers. They lobbied for and manipulated immigration laws to import immigrant workers—Chinese, Japanese, Filipinos, and Mexicans—whom they hired for miserably low wages.

Jessie Lopez De La Cruz is one of those workers. Born in 1919 in California, she is Mexican American—Chicana.* All her life she has been a farmworker. She is small, compact, sturdy. Her face has the flat planes, deepset eyes, and straight, jet eyelashes of the *Indios*—Native American ancestors in Mexico. For nearly twenty years, since her children have been grown, she has been a union militant, a community activist, a translator, an educator, and a star witness in hearings on farm-labor conditions and land monopoly. On picket lines, she has been sprayed with pesticides, run at by growers' trucks, and shot at.

Come to her house and Jessie De La Cruz will feed you. While you eat, neighbors and relatives will knock at the door, coming in for advice, conversation, a cup of coffee. "With us," she says, "family is very important. When my sister died, I took care of her children, and when my nephew's wife died, I took care of their children." Gradually, it becomes clear that Jessie De La Cruz's political activism has some of its deepest roots in her ties with friends and families.

---

* Chicano/Chicana used to be a somewhat pejorative term. In the sixties, it was seized back in race pride, particularly by young Mexican Americans, much as the term "black" was seized back by Afro-Americans.

Look away from the photographs of family, let your attention wander a minute from the conversations going on around you: you'll notice a poster on the wall opposite you, just above the space heater. A line of pastel-shirted, brown-skinned people with tall white hats are rushing across the poster in profile. If you ask Jessie who they are, she'll tell you they're the *Zapatistas*, followers of Emiliano Zapata, the great Mexican land reformer and revolutionary who fought for the peasantry in the early years of the century. Look to the wall just behind you and you'll see a burlap rectangle studded with countless buttons: HUELGA! (Strike); NFWA (National Farmworkers' Association); MAY DAY, INTERNATIONAL WORKERS' DAY; BOYCOTT GALLO WINE; SI SE PUEDE (Yes, We Can); VIETNAM VETERANS AGAINST THE WAR. Under the burlap, on a table, stands a photograph of George and Eleanor McGovern, which reminds you that Jessie De La Cruz was a delegate to the 1972 Democratic convention.

De La Cruz did not begin political work until the age of forty-two. But from childhood on, she was aware of the exploitative relations between big growers and the workers who toiled in their fields. Like so many millions of Mexican Americans, she grew up in a family of migrant workers. Migrant workers travel—or migrate—around the country in search of work. As the crops ripen from early spring until late fall, the workers follow them—hoeing beets, picking other vegetables and fruits, chopping and thinning cotton. Often, whole families migrate, following the crops, working from dawn to sunset stooped over in the fields. Until the United Farmworkers union helped to better conditions of life and labor for these workers, they were desperately poor; their pay during the growing season was often not enough to live on through the winter. Jessie De La Cruz's husband, Arnold, remembers getting ten cents an hour in 1933. "Three dollars for a twelve-hour day was good," he says. "Before it was $1.40."

As a child, Jessie traveled the annual circuit from Anaheim (near Disneyland) up to the Santa Clara Valley in northern California with her family. "We'd come north to San José sometime in August to pick prunes, then start back. We'd stop in the San Joaquin Valley to pick grapes, and then go south to

Arvin for the cotton. In November or December, we'd come back to the Los Angeles area and we'd stay there till the next season." Like other farmworkers' children, she got shifted from school to school as the family went in search of work. Like others, she was forced to stop school early: she reached the sixth grade.

In 1933, the family moved permanently to the San Joaquin Valley. From then until 1956, when Jessie De La Cruz moved to Fresno with her husband, home base was a series of labor camps. The cabins in the farmworkers' camps were twelve by fifteen feet—very small for families of ten or more. From the outside, the houses looked like little more than shacks. They had tarpaper roofs and uninsulated board walls that you could stick your fingers through, the cracks were so large. Boxes along dusty roads, the houses went on for miles and miles.

Jessie's father left her mother with three girls to rear when Jessie, the oldest of the daughters, was nine. Her maternal grandparents and her mother cared for her and her mother's younger brothers, whom she looked on as her own brothers. When she was ten, her mother and grandfather died, leaving her grandmother in charge of the entire family.

Jessie Lopez married Arnold De La Cruz in 1938. Between 1939 and 1947 she bore six children—four sons and two daughters. She raised an adopted daughter, the child of a sister who died. All of her children have been politically active in the union and in community activities.

In 1962, Cesar Chavez, who came from a background almost identical to Jessie Lopez De La Cruz's, founded the National Farmworkers' Association (later to become the United Farmworkers). The union was the first to organize farmworkers successfully. From the start, it concentrated not only on higher wages, shorter hours, and other on-the-job gains, but just as importantly on principles of racial dignity and social justice. The union also worked for better health care and other social services. Most of the union's leaders came from the same origins as the women and men they organized, and no union staff member earned more than five dollars a week. The idealism of the union and the ways it went about its work made it

more than just another union. Its followers called it *La Causa*—
the Cause.

Shortly after the union was established, Cesar Chavez came
to the De La Cruz's home to talk to them about the organization and to ask them to join it. It was then, in 1962, that Jessie
De La Cruz began her work for the union. She was the first
woman to organize people in the fields during working hours.
She did this and other union work until 1968, when she was
put in charge of the United Farmworkers (UFW) hiring hall
in Parlier, a little town southeast of Fresno. By then, she was
well-known for her courage on picket lines; for her endless
patience with those she organized; for her firm convictions; for
her no-nonsense, razor-sharp comebacks in public debates with
big growers and their allies.

Jessie De La Cruz has long served as a bilingual translator at
meetings, conferences, government hearings, and in encounters
between farmworkers and growers. She has been active in a
host of community organizations and has been an adviser to the
state's Commission on the Status of Women. She is secretary-
treasurer of National Land for People, an organization that has
been working to break up land monopolies on the west side of
the San Joaquin Valley, so that families like the De La Cruzes
may buy plots of land there.

Together with three other farmworker families, Jessie and
Arnold De La Cruz have bought forty acres of land near Fresno,
which they work cooperatively. She is constantly called upon
to talk with people and testify in government hearings about
land ownership for small farmers, about cooperative farming,
about the fight against the big corporations on the west side of
the Valley. Her life and work combine a tough stubborness with
optimism and humility. "Sometimes," she says, "I just feel
thankful for the path that has been opened to me to help people,
trying to open new doors."

Rootedness and Uprooting

We have pounded our hands in despair
against the adobe walls,

for our inheritance . . . is lost and dead.
The shields of our warriors were its defense,
but they could not save it.

We have chewed dry twigs and salt grasses:
We have filled our mouths with dust and bits of adobe:
We have eaten lizards, rats and worms.

—From the Aztec, upon the conquest of that
nation by the Spanish invaders.

In 1910, 96.6 percent of rural families were landless in Mexico, and the small working class of the cities was impoverished. Revolution broke out that year. Even though Mexico had won its independence from Spain nearly a century before, its own ruling class ran the country, and United States business interests controlled much of the country's wealth. The majority of Mexican people worked either on huge estates—*haciendas*—owned by a few large landowners, or in city industries. Under the great revolutionaries, Emiliano Zapata and Pancho Villa, it seemed for a time that the poor would reap the benefits of the revolution. Zapata and Villa called in particular for the breaking up of the huge *haciendas*. They wanted the land to be redistributed among the *Indios*, the peasantry. But although Porfirio Diaz, a dictator ruling the country since 1867, was overthrown in 1910, the government that finally was established at the revolution's close in 1920 was no better than Diaz's had been. In 1920, United States business still held major shares of the country's wealth—and the poor people of Mexico continued to grow poorer.

A great migration began. Thousands of men and women, their *Indio* heritage showing in the color of their skin, in the slight upward tilt of their dark eyes, came north across the Mexican border to the United States. Families came to where there was work—laying railroad tracks; toiling in mines; working in the fields stooped over twelve hours and more a day, often in temperatures of more than a hundred degrees.

Newly arrived in the States, Jessie Lopez De La Cruz's grandfather worked on the railroad, then in mining. Next, he came to

Anaheim where he found work in a cement factory that made pipes for irrigation. For a while, the family lived in a house the grandfather built. Then, disaster brought that security to an end, and the family began traveling the crop circuit as migrant workers.

In 1929, the Great Depression began. Between 1930 and 1933, the number of unemployed in the United States rose from four million to more than thirteen million. Chicanos were especially hard-hit. They were forced to compete for work with other desperate farmworkers, refugees from Oklahoma and Arkansas driven out of those states by a whirlwind of dust storms that buried houses, crops, machines, and animals in its fury.

Between 1929 and 1930, personal tragedy hit Jessie Lopez De La Cruz's family. Jessie's three-year-old sister was burned to death in an accident in 1929. In March 1930, her mother died of cancer. Three months later, in June, the grandfather she loved so dearly also died. The family lived in Fresno, then moved to Watts—a working-class suburb of Los Angeles. In 1933, they moved north permanently to the San Joaquin Valley, where they spent their time among a number of labor camps, working the crops.

My grandmother was born in Mexico in Aguas Calientes, near Guadalajara. She was raised by a very strict father and she married at thirteen. That was the custom. The girls, as soon as they were old enough to learn cooking and sewing, would get married. Most married at twelve or thirteen. My grandmother married and she was left out in a little shack by herself. She was so young, so afraid. . . .

She had my mother and my oldest brother when she and my grandfather came across.* My grandfather worked for the railroad laying the ties and tracks. Then he worked for a mining company. After that we moved to Anaheim. We lived in a big four-bedroom house my grandfather built. With my grand-

---

* Jessie De La Cruz calls her uncles "brothers." After the age of ten, she was raised by her grandmother, and some of her mother's brothers weren't much older than she was.

parents and their children, three children of my mother's sister who had died, and the three of us, that made a big crowd.

My grandfather would get up Sunday mornings and start the fire in a great big wood-burning stove. He would wrap us up in blankets and seat us around that stove on chairs and say, "Now, don't get too close to the stove. Take care of the younger children." Then he would go out to the store and get bananas and oranges and cereal that he'd cook for us to eat, and milk, and he would feed us Sunday mornings.

My grandmother had a beautiful garden—carnations and pansies and roses, and a big bush of bleeding heart. She was very proud of that. My grandfather used to grow a vegetable garden in back of our house; we had a large yard. And I remember that while he was working for the company, he got us one of those big cement pipes with a hole in the bottom. He would plug that up with a piece of wood he carved to fit the hole, and then he would fill this up with water. My brothers and I would get into it. We had a grand time with that!

But then, I remember, there was a flood one night. We were all scared, and we were crying because it was raining very hard and water and oil from some oil wells around there were just running down the streets into homes. There was oil all over, inside the house. My grandfather and the older children and neighbors had lanterns and shovels, and they were piling up mud to keep the water from going into our houses. We were taken to the second floor of a store. Many families spent the night there. The next day, when we went home, my grandmother cried because her flowers were all gone—full of oil and mud.

Then my grandfather had an accident. The middle finger of his right hand was crushed, and he couldn't work for about two weeks. When he went back he was told that he'd already been replaced by another worker. So he was out of a job. He decided we'd better go on and pick the crops. We had done that before, during the summer. But this time we went for good.

We came north. The families got together; the women would start cooking at night, boiling eggs and potatoes and making piles of tortillas and tacos, and these lunches would be packed in pails and boxes. There was as much fruit as they could get together, and roasted pumpkin seeds. My uncle had a factory where he made Mexican candy in East Los Angeles. And he used to give us a lot of pumpkin seeds. So my mother dried these, and she roasted and salted them for the trip to keep the drivers awake. We'd start in a car caravan, six or seven families together, one car watching for the other, and when it got a little dark they'd pull onto the roadside and build a fire and start some cooking to feed us. Then they'd spread blankets and quilts on the ground, and we would sleep there that night. The next morning, the women and older children would get up first and start the breakfast. And we smaller children, it was our job to fold the blankets and put them back in the cars and trucks. Then my brothers and the men would check the cars over again, and after breakfast all the women would wash the dishes and pack them, get 'em in the cars, and we'd start again.

We'd finally get to Delano and we would work there a little.* If work was scarce, we would keep on going till San José. I did the same thing my mother and my grandfather and my uncles did, picking prunes on our hands and knees off the ground, and putting them in the buckets. We were paid four dollars a ton, and we had to fill forty boxes to make it a ton. They made us sign a contract that we would stay there until all the prunes were picked. When we would finish the prunes, in early September, we would start back. And stop on the way to Mendota to pick cotton.

When I was about thirteen, I used to lift a twelve-foot sack of cotton with 104 or 112 pounds. When you're doing this work, you get to be an expert. I could get that sack and put it on my shoulder, and walk with that sack for about a city block or maybe a little less, to where the scale was. I could hook this sack up on the scale, have it weighed, take it off the hook, and put it back on my shoulder; and walk up a ladder about eight-feet high and dump all that cotton in the trailer.

My brothers taught me how to do it. When I first started

---

* Delano is northeast of Los Angeles near the bottom of the San Joaquin Valley. It was in Delano that the great grape strike called by Cesar Chavez's National Farmworkers' Association, together with Larry Itliong's United Farm-workers' Organizing Committee, began in 1965.

picking cotton, they had to untie their sack and go on my side of the row and help me put this sack on my shoulder, so they taught me how to do it when it was full. It's stiff. My brother said, "Just walk over it, pick up one end, and sort of pull it up, up, and then bend, and when the middle of the sack hits your shoulder, you just stand up slowly. Then put your arm on your waist, and the sack will sit on your shoulder and you can just walk with it." At thirteen, fourteen, I was lifting 104 and 112 pounds. I weighed ninety-five, I guess!

As a child, I remember we had tents without any floors. It was Giffen's Camp Number Nine. I remember the water coming from under the tent at night to where we were sleeping. My brothers would get up with shovels and put mud around the tent to keep the water out. But our blankets and our clothes were always damp during the winter.

There were truckloads that got brought in, of little blocks of wood from some lumber company. People could go out and get some of those for heating or for cooking in those oil drums or woodburning stoves, if they happened to have one. We had an oil drum. There were too many people and not enough wood to go around, so my brothers would have to go out and hunt for something to burn in the stove so we could cook.

There was a lot of disease. I don't remember two weeks out of my life: I had typhoid fever. I was put in the hospital in Bakersfield. At that time, we lived in some kind of tin building where they stored grain and apricot after it's been dried, and raisins. During the winter, I recall, I'd get up in the morning and want to wash my hands and face. We had to run quite a distance to the water faucet. I'd open the faucet and no water would come out: it was frozen. There was a barrel underneath with just a block of ice on the top. I would break this with my hands and wash my face and hands in a hurry and run back to the house and get ready for school. And in this water you'd see little things crawling up and going down. I don't know what they're called. But the typhoid is from water that's standing too long in one place, like this barrel, where my brothers and sisters and the other kids washed.

At Di Giorgio, another big camp, one of the big growers that the United Farmworkers were fighting for a time, my little sister was burned to death in a fire, an accident. It was 1929, and then in 1930 my mother died: I think she had cancer but we don't know. I remember waking at night and hearing her cry, just in pain, you know. I'd start crying under the blankets, and my grandmother would come and say, "No, don't cry, just be quiet, your mama's gonna be all right." My grandmother would get water as hot as she could and dip towels in it and put it on my mother's back where she had this pain. My grandmother took my mother to the county hospital, and when she got back I didn't recognize my mother. Her hair had been cut short above her ears and she was thin; her eyes were sunken; I just didn't know her. I was crying all the time. She finally died in March: I wasn't ten yet. And then in June my grandfather died—same year. It was very hard for my grandmother. She had seven children. And then my sister and myself made it nine.

We had some very hard times. In 1930, a friend of my grandmother gave her some money. She got some *menudos* (tripe) and hominy. She said, "Take out those pots and soak this." She soaked the tripe, added garlic. The next day, she got my brother to go with her with a little cart. She went from house to house selling *menudo*. The money she raised from that, she'd buy more. She'd use what was left over to feed us. There was no wood for heating. And one time, to top it off, we all got scarlet fever: they put a sign on our door. Nobody was to go in or out.

We'd go out on the hilltop and pick mushrooms, mustard greens. My brothers would kill wild rabbits. And this we would eat during the winter.

In '33, we came up north to follow the crops because my brothers couldn't find any work in Los Angeles during the Depression. I remember going hungry to school. I didn't have a sweater. I had nothing. I'd come to school and they'd want to know, "What did you have for breakfast?" They gave us a paper, to write down what we had! I *invented* things! We had eggs and milk, I'd say, and the same things the other kids would write, I'd write. There weren't many Mexican people at school, mostly whites, and I'd watch to see what they were writing or the pictures that they'd show. You know: glasses of milk, and toast, and oranges and bananas and cereal. I'd never had *anything*. My grandmother couldn't work, we couldn't work, so we went hungry. One of my friends at school said, "Jessie, why don't you eat with us?" And I said, "I don't have any money. So they talked to the teacher, and the teacher called me one day during recess. She said, "Jessie, where's your father?"

"I don't have one."

"Where's your mother?"

"I don't have one." Then she wanted to know who did I live with. I said my grandmother and my uncles and aunts. She said, "Did you eat any breakfast?"

"No."

"Did your brothers and sisters eat breakfast?"

"No."

"Did you bring a lunch?"

"No." So she said, "Well, you help us in the kitchen. You can help us clear the tables after all the children eat, and you and your brothers and sisters can come and eat." It got to where after school, everything that was left in those big pots they'd put in those gallon cans for tomato sauce or canned peaches, and say, "You can take these home with you." And I'd take them home and we'd have a party—my grandmother and everybody.

From there we moved again, this time to Dohenny Park, which is by the sea by San Juan Capistrano near Clemente. Sundays my grandmother would take us for walks. She'd take my sisters and some of our girlfriends, and we'd go hiking up those mountains and see all sorts of flowers and cactuses. We'd pick up all these wildflowers and just run out in the fields. Oh! I loved that.

We weren't feeling sorry for ourselves: we didn't know there was anything better than what we had. Everybody that came into the camp and stayed there lived the way we did. In the summer of 1934, this family came in and they had a radio. Boy! We had to make friends with those girls! One Sunday these girls came over to my house and asked if I could get my grandmother to let me go over to their house. I asked her. She said, "What do you want to visit them for?"

"Well, it's Julia and her sister and these other girls, they want me to go, and they were asking me. Would you let me?"

"Okay. But I'll be outside watching. Are there any boys there?"

"No, just girls. They have a radio and we want to listen to it." So we got this radio into an empty cabin where nobody lived. There were seven or eight girls and we danced with that radio. I guess our parents thought we should have a little fun because my brother came in one night and said, "Guess who's here? Doña Petra Moreno." She was from back home when my grandfather and my mother were living. We met them that night. Doña Petra Moreno had three boys, and they were musicians. One played the guitar, another the violin, and one played the banjo. It got to where during the summer we would string up lights around these empty cabins and the boys would play and the families would dance—the teen-agers and the parents and everybody! Then we were having a good time!

Courtship, Marriage, and Childrearing

Oh, hard is the fortune of all womankind,
They're always controlled, they're always confined . . .

—*North American folksong.*

Mexican American women of Jessie De La Cruz's generation grew up as her grandmother had. From childhood, they learned that women were not free to come and go as men were, and that women had three jobs—housework, childbearing and rearing, and fieldwork. "Before I married," says De La Cruz, "I worked *every* day, Saturday and Sunday, too. Sometimes my brothers would tell me, 'You stay home on Saturday and we gonna come home at noon. By the time we get here you have our clothes pressed and cleaned and shoes shined and we'll take you to the dance.' So," she laughs, reminiscing, "I was supposed to get up in the morning and after they ate breakfast they'd go to work and I'd stay behind. I'd do the washing, I had to starch their shirts and I had to iron them just so."

Jessie met Arnold when she was fourteen: they married five years later. After a year of marriage, Arnold began staying away nights and leaving Jessie alone, as her grandfather had left her grandmother before her. One day she took a stand for her own rights at home—the first in a series.

Childbearing, childrearing, work in the camps, wringing a living from the earth—Jessie De La Cruz made connections between these experiences and larger social issues all along the way. They were to become the foundations of her later political work.

When I was a girl, boys were allowed to go out and have friends and visit there in the camp, and even go to town. But the girls—the mother was always watching them. We couldn't talk to nobody. If I had a boyfriend, he had to send me letters, drop notes on his way or send them along with somebody. We did no dating. We weren't allowed to. If girls came to visit at my house, my grandmother sat right there to listen to what we were talking about. We weren't allowed to speak English because she couldn't understand, and she would say, "How can I tell if you're talking about me or if you're fighting or something?" This is what I mean by sheltered. We were allowed nowhere except out to the field, and then we always worked between my two older brothers. One brother was on one side, and me next, then my two sisters, and then my next oldest brother on the other end. And we were not allowed to talk. The only one they trusted was Arnold. He's the one I married. He was allowed to come in our house any time of day. He was always joking and talking with my grandmother. Nights, he would come in and sit on the floor with us. I'd always have some songbooks, and he'd pick one up and look at it, and take out a pencil and start writing. He was writing me a note, and then he'd close the book and say, "Have you learned this song?" And he'd open the book for me to read and I'd read the note right in front of my grandmother! So now I understand the saying, where there is a will there's a way.

I was fourteen when I met Arnold, in 1933. We lived next door to his family, which was a big one. I'd go there and help Arnold's mother make stacks of tortillas. She didn't have time enough to do all the work for the little children. I'd go and help her. When she went to the hospital in 1935, when Arnold's younger brother was born, I cared for the whole family. I'd make tortillas and cook. The little ones we kept in our house, and the rest of them stayed in their cabin.

Arnold and I got married in 1938 in Firebaugh, where we'd all moved. We had a big party with an orchestra: some of Arnold's friends played the violin and guitar. But we had no honeymoon. On the second day after our wedding, he went back to his job—irrigating. I'd get up at four o'clock in the morning to fix his breakfast and his lunch. He'd start the fire for me. I did the cooking in his mother's kitchen. We had three cabins in all by this time. His mother had one cabin that was used as a bedroom. There was ours. And the other cabin in front was used as the kitchen for all of us. So in the morning I'd get up and run across and I'd fix his breakfast and his lunch and he'd go off and I'd go back to bed. He'd come home about four or five o'clock and there would be ice around his ears. It didn't come from the irrigating. It came from riding in the pickup. They were going fast, and the wind was that cold! He'd come home and get next to the stove where the fire was burning and have something hot to eat. He worked twelve hours a day.

I felt I was overworked in the house. I felt like saying, "Okay, there's the whole thing, you take care of it," but I couldn't. I felt, "What can Arnold's mother do without the help I'm giving her?" I felt sorry for her. She'd worked very hard and she had so many children, and had to wash her clothes in a tub with a rock board and do the ironing by heating the irons on top of the stove. All of us had to do this, but not many families had eight or nine little children.

I cooked with her until May. But I kept after Arnold: "I want my own kitchen!" So in May we drove all the way into Fresno. We got a few spoons and plates and pots and skillets, and I started my own housekeeping. I still went to his mother's to help her during the day when Arnold was working. But I cooked in my own stove.

After I was married, sometime in May, my husband was chopping cotton and I said, "I want to go with you."

"You can't! You have to stay at home!"

"I just feel like going outside somewhere. I haven't gone anyplace. I want to at least go out to the fields. Take another hoe and I'll help you." I went, but only for one or two days. Then he refused to take me. He said, "You have to stay home and raise children." I was pregnant with my first one. "I want you to rest," he said. "You're not supposed to work. You worked ever since I can remember. Now that you're married, you are going to rest." So I stayed home, but I didn't call it rest doing all the cooking for his mother.

Arnold was raised in the old Mexican custom—men on the one side, women on the other. Women couldn't do anything. Your husband would say, "Go here," you'd do it. You didn't dare go out without your husband saying you could.

Arnold never beat me, or anything like that. But every time I used to talk to him he didn't answer, even if I asked a question. He'd say, "Well, you don't have to know about it." If I asked, "Arnold, has the truck been paid for?" he wouldn't answer. Or I would ask him, "Did you pay the loan company?" he wouldn't answer. Then I'd get kind of mad and say, "Why can't you tell me?" and he'd say, "What do you want to know about it, are you going to pay for it, or what? Let me do the worrying." Now that is all changed; we talk things over. But in the beginning it was different.

The first year we were married, he was home every night. After the first year was up, I guess that was the end of the honeymoon. He would just take off, and I wouldn't see him for three or four days, even more. I didn't even ask, "Where were you?" I accepted it. I wasn't supposed to question him. He would come in and take his dirty clothes off, pile them up, and when I did the wash the next day I'd look through his pockets and find bus ticket stubs of where he'd been to—Santa Maria, miles and miles away from home. He would be home for about two days and

(text continued on page 114)

FARMWORKERS' ORGANIZER

Far right: Jessie Lopez De La Cruz pruning plums. **1:** De La Cruz picking grapes, 1972. **2:** De La Cruz speaking to farmworkers in the fields. **3:** Jessie and Arnold De La Cruz with some of their children and grandchildren. **4:** Jessie De La Cruz speaking at a United Farmworkers meeting. **5:** De La Cruz at a union rally. **6:** Lifting cartons of fruit. **7:** Jessie and Arnold De La Cruz working in the fields. **8:** Jessie De La Cruz at a United Farmworkers march.

JESSIE LOPEZ DE LA CRUZ

BOYCOTT GALLO!

then take off again with his friends, his pals who were gambling. I really couldn't blame him that much, because when he was young, before we were married, he was never even allowed to go to a dance. So he was trying out his wings.

After a time I said, "I have really had it. Why do you have to go with your friends all the time when I'm being left alone?"

"Well, what's wrong with that? You can go visit my mother." I said, "Big deal, you want me to go visit your mother and help make some tortillas." So he finally started giving me money, five or six dollars. He'd say, "My mother's going to Fresno. If you want to go with them you can go." Or he would say, "Doña Genoveva," a friend of ours, "is going to Fresno and she said you can come along." I'd get my kids—I had two of them—ready early in the morning and we'd go to Fresno or to visit her husband, who was up in the mountains in the hospital for TB. One day I just said, "Why do I have to depend on other people to take me out somewhere? I'm married, I have a husband—who should be taking me out." The next time he was home and said, "Here's the money," I said, "I don't want to go." He let it go at that, and I did, too. I didn't say another word. The following weekend he said, "Do you want to go to a show? My mother's going. They're going to Fresno." I said, "No." Then about the third time this happened he said, "Why don't you want to go anymore?"

"I do, I do want to go. I want to go somewhere, but not with anyone else. I want to go with you." So then he started staying home and he'd say, "Get ready, we're going into Fresno." And both of us would come in, bring the children, go to a show and eat, or just go to the park.

We'd come in about once a month and bring the children with us. They just loved that, and now they're always talking about it, how Arnold would sing funny songs for them all the way from camp to town, and we'd all have a good time. This began happening around 1942, when I was in my twenties.

Arnold would never teach me how to drive. One day I asked him to. We were on a ditch bank about eight-feet wide. He says, "Get on the driver's side. Now, turn around and go back." I got out. I said, "*You* do it! Just tell me you don't want me to learn if that's what you want." Then in 1947 I asked my sister, Margaret, and she showed me. We practiced in a field. After a few times she said, "Hey! You know how to drive! Let's go into town so you can buy your groceries."

So one day I said to Arnold, "I'm going out to get the groceries."

"Who's going to take you?"

"Me. Maggie taught me how to drive and it's about time I learned. I stay home and cook for all these men"—I was cooking in a boarding house in the camp at the time—"and if I run short I have to send for someone to go get it, and they never give me back my change. So I'm going to do the buying from now on."

Before I was married, in 1933, we would come and camp by the river in that place where we were picking grapes. After I was married, we still kept on coming there to pick grapes. We would get a blanket and tie it to the limbs of one of the trees, and to the chicken wire fence that divided the horses and cows and rabbits from us. We would sleep under this tree and do our cooking there and fight the flies. For walls, we used what they called sweat boxes. They're about the size of a three-by-five table. After the grapes are dried out in rows, they're picked up and put into sweat boxes. I would nail some of these together as a wall for privacy. Some I would place on the ground and put our mattress on top for a bed. By turning two boxes right side down, and a third on top right side up, I would fill the top one with dirt and put three rocks in a triangle. That would be our stove, where I would cook our meals.

Sometimes there were about twenty families camped the whole stretch of the riverbank. I'd do my washing there. If there was a big rock, we would scrub our clothes there. I'd get a tub and I'd put some water in it, and then I'd put the soap in there and I'd scrub the soap on the shirts or whatever, and I'd scrub on the rub board. When I first started, at around twelve, I got blisters on my knuckles, but later my grandmother taught me how to use the scrub board, and after that it was easy.

Of course I didn't wash sheets. We didn't have them. Pillow cases we didn't have. We just had the blankets, which I'd made out of flour sacks made of cotton. When I found out that I was pregnant with my first child, I didn't have anything to make clothes for him, so out of old shirts or flour sacks or whatever little pieces of material I could get, I used to make clothes I knew he was going to need. Then the next one came. Friends, after their babies had outgrown these clothes, they would give them to me, and then I'd pass them on to a neighbor that was having a baby. We always tried to help each other.

My first child was born in 1939, Ray. I had five more. I also took Susan, the girl my sister left when she died. Now I have fourteen grandchildren, and this spring it will be fifteen, sometime in May.

I stopped working toward the last months of my pregnancies, but I would start again after they were born. When I was working and I couldn't find somebody, I would take them with me. I started taking Ray with me when he wasn't a year old yet. I'd carry one of those big washtubs and put it under the vine and sit him there. I knew he was safe; he couldn't climb out. Arnold and I would move the tub along with us as we worked. I hated to leave him with somebody that probably wouldn't take care of him the way I could.

Once there was nearly an accident with Susan. It was when we were picking cotton. You know, you're picking the cotton and putting it in the sack, which is tied around your waist. When it got kind of full I used to put Susan right in the back and pull her along with my cotton. But then she got sleepy—she was a little over a year when we were picking cotton. I would get her blanket and put it ahead on the row—almost way out there by the end—lay her down and give her her bottle, and by the time we got finished picking up to where she was, then it would be time to go home. So one time I left her; I felt I wasn't too far away. I could hear her if she cried; it was silent although people were working. Then I saw this truck coming. It had a trailer hitched to it—not on the road where it was supposed to be, but on top of the cotton rows. My cotton sack was too full for me to lift up and run with it! There were about seventy-five pounds of cotton in there. I tried to untie it, but instead I made a knot in it, I was that nervous, yelling and crying! Arnold was trying to untie his sack, too. I called to one friend, kept shouting to the man in the truck to stop. By the time I got loose from the sack and got out there the truck had almost run over her. I said, "Never again will I put her out there!"

In 1944 we moved to a labor camp in Huron and we stayed there till 1956. But before that we had a single-room cabin. I used to separate the bed section from the kitchen by nailing blankets or pieces of canvas to divide. We had our bed and another bed for the children. All the boys slept in the bed, and the girl slept with us in our bed. During the night, Bobby being the youngest of the boys would wake up and be scared, and he always ended up in our bed! It was pretty crowded, but what could you do? I was always nailing orange crates on the walls to use as cupboards for dishes. Then I had a man build a cupboard for me. It had four shelves and a screen door to keep the flies out. The dishes I didn't use every day I kept there. Like if I happened to buy a cake plate, you know, those big ones with the long stem, I'd put it in there. I never had a set of dishes. I'd get pretty teacups I didn't want to use every day and put them in that cupboard. The rest went into those boxes.

Once, I remember, it was wintertime. We were so crowded, and I couldn't send the kids out to play. Night after night I kept saying, "You better go to sleep. It's late." But they'd be jumping up and down on the bed, which was on one side of my cupboard. I'd say, "Go to sleep. You're going to break my dishes." They'd be quiet for a little while, and start all over again. It finally happened. One day they knocked my cupboard over and broke all my dishes. I sat down and cried. I couldn't help it. I sat down on top of all that broken glass and said, "I'm going to run away. You won't mind me, you just won't do things when I ask you. You broke all my dishes. You'll never see me again! I'm going to run away!" They all started crying and hugging me. "Mama! Don't go!" Then I felt bad. How could I do this to them? "No," I said, "I'm not going to run away. But you have to mind me." They still remember that.

There was a lot of sickness. I remember when my kids got whooping cough. Arnold would come back late in the evening and wet, and the children were coughing and coughing. Arnold was sick, too, he was burning hot. During this time instead of staying in my own cabin at night I'd go to my mother-in-law's. The children would wake up at night coughing and there was blood coming out of their noses. I cried and cried, I was afraid they'd choke. I went to the clinic and they told me the children had whooping cough. That cough lasted six months.

I had a little girl who died in '43. She was so tiny . . . only five months. The cause was the way we were living, under the tree, with only chicken wire to separate us from the cows and horses. There were thousands of flies. I didn't have a refrigerator, no place to refrigerate the milk. She got sick. I couldn't stop the diarrhea. They told me she had a brain infection. And so I had to leave her, and my little girl died. We were so poor and I felt so helpless—there was nothing I could do.

It was like that for all of us. I would see babies who died. It was claimed if you lifted a young baby up fast, the soft spot would cave in and it would get diarrhea and dehydrate and die. After all these years I know it wasn't that that killed them. It was hunger, malnutrition, no money to pay the doctors. When the union came, this was one of the things we fought against.

Work in the Fields

I'd been trained as a child that the woman just walked behind the husband and kept quiet, no matter what the husband does. But in work I've been equal to men since I was a child, working alongside men, doing the same hard work and earning the same wages.

—Jessie De La Cruz.

"What I am telling you," said Jessie De La Cruz to a group of senators in a hearing several years ago, "is not only my history . . . all farmworkers have gone through this." Nor is her story of work at home and in the fields hers alone: millions of Chicanas have gotten up at four in the morning to fix breakfast for their husbands as Jessie did for Arnold. Millions have worked in the fields save in the late stages of pregnancy and the early months of their infants' lives.

In the fields, Jessie De La Cruz picked grapes and apricots and hoed beets. For seventeen years of their married lives—from 1939 to 1956—the De La Cruzes chopped and thinned cotton, living on the land of Russell Giffen, the San Joaquin Valley's cotton baron. "I measured Mr. Giffen's land by the inch because I worked with an eight-inch hoe, ten hours a day, getting $7.35 after deduction, out of ten hours of work," Jessie De La Cruz said in the same Senate hearing. When there was no work in Giffen's cotton, the De La Cruz family would travel from their home base at one or another of Russell Giffen's labor camps and work other crops.

Jessie De La Cruz did other work, too. From 1944 to 1956, when the family was in a Giffen camp at Huron, a little town southwest of Fresno, one of her jobs was cooking in a boarding house, feeding dozens of men. She also had a lunch wagon. She would get up at four in the morning; cook for the men; make the lunches; then take the wagon out to the fields and sell tacos, hamburgers, doughnuts.

From 1939 until 1944, we stayed at Giffen's camp number three. We were still following the crops. We would go out to pick cotton or apricots or grapes here near Fresno, or we would go farther north to Tracey to pick peas. When there was no work chopping or picking cotton, we'd go to Patterson or San José to pick apricots. Arnold did the picking and I did cutting for the drying-out in the sheds. The apricots would be picked out in the field or in the orchard. They'd bring 'em in, in trucks, and they'd just set them beside us. They always had a boy or two that would dump these apricots on a table. We would have a knife, and we'd cut around it and take out the pit, and just spread them out on top of big trays. After we filled all these trays, they would come and take these out where they were dried. And they'd put some more on the table on the trays for us to cut.

We always went where the women and men were going to work, because if it were just the men working it wasn't worth going out there because we wouldn't earn enough to support a family. In one camp we were living at, the camp was at the edge of a cotton patch and the cotton needed to be thinned. We would start early. It was May. It got so hot, we would start around 6:30 A.M. and work for four or five hours, then walk home and eat and rest until about three-thirty in the afternoon when it cooled off. We would go back and work until we couldn't see. Then we'd get home and rest, visit, talk. Then I'd clean up the kitchen. I was doing the housework and working out in the fields and taking care of the kids. I had two children by this time.

Other times we would pick grapes. The sand is very hot. It gets up to about a hundred-eight, a hundred-ten degrees during the summer out in the fields. We wore tennis shoes to protect our feet from the hot sand. I'd get a pan and put it under the vine and cut the grapes. The grower wanted us to cut them, not pull them. You had to hold the grape bunches gently—not to crush the grapes—in your hand, and you'd have to use your knife to cut off from the stem and place the grapes in a pan. After that pan was full, you would spread these grapes in a paper tray where the sun was shining. But I was using my knife this way, and kept on cutting and cutting toward me, and these knives have a hook on them, and the handle is kind of rounded. One day I came to a real hard one. The stem was drying so I had to use a lot of strength, and this knife gave me a big cut on my neck. It scared me! Arnold said to just sit down and stay there. He washed the blood off. That was my first experience working out in the field after I married.

The hardest work we did was thinning beets. You were required to use a short-handled hoe. The cutting edge is about seven- to eight-inches wide, and the handle is about a foot long. You have to be bent over with the hoe in one hand. You walk down the rows stooped over. You have to work hard, fast, as fast as you can because you were paid by the row, not by the hour. I learned how to do it without straining my back too much. I put my hand on my left knee, and I got so good at it that I'd leave one beet on each stroke. You're supposed to pull one off with your hand if you leave two. I'd go as fast as I could and I'd always leave one and one.Most of them would be chopping, and then picking and separating with two hands. But I was walking backward and going fast. But when I wanted to stand up, I'd have to go very slow and I couldn't stand up straight. I still have a bad back, and I think I got it from the short-handled hoe.

I also used a short-handled hoe in the lettuce fields. The lettuce grows in a bed. You work in little furrows between two rows. First you thin them with the hoe, then you pick off the tops. My brothers-in-law and Arnold and I and some other friends worked there picking the tops off the lettuce. By the time they had taken up one row, I had taken up two. The men would go between the two beds and take one row and break the little balls off. But I took two rows at a time, one with each hand. By the time I finished my two rows at the other end, it was close to a mile long, and my brother-in-law had only taken one row part-way. He said, "I'm quitting! If Jessie can beat me at this kind of work, I'm no good at it." So he never came back. About three or four other men wouldn't go back to work because they were beaten by a woman. They said, "I'm ashamed to have a woman even older than I am work faster than I can. This is women's job." I said, "Hey! What do you mean? You mean the men's job is washing dishes and baking tortillas?" They said working out in the fields is women's work because we were faster at it!

Out in the fields there were never any restrooms. We had to go eight or ten hours without relief. If there wasn't brush or a little ditch, we were forced to wait until we got home! Just the women. The men didn't need to pull their clothes down. Later, when I worked for the Farmworkers, in a hearing I said, "I was working for Russell Giffen, the biggest grower in Huron. These big growers have a lot of money because we earned all that money for them. Because of our sweat and our labor that we put on the land. What they do instead of supplying restrooms and clean water where we can wash our hands, is put posts on the ground with a piece of gunny sack wound around them." That's where we went. And that thing was moved along with us. It was just four stakes stuck in the ground, and then there was canvas or a piece of gunny sack around it. You would be working, and this restroom would be right there. The canvas didn't come up high enough in front for privacy. We made it a practice to go two at a time. One would stand outdoors and watch outside that nobody came along. And then the other would do the same for the one inside. Then we'd go back to work.

La Causa

I worked in your orchards of peaches and fruits,
Slept on the ground in the light of your moon;
On the edge of your cities you've seen us and then
We come with the dust and we go with the wind . . .

Green pastures of plenty from dry desert ground
From the Grand Coolie Dam where the water runs down
Every state in the union us migrants have been,
We've worked in this fight and we'll fight till we win.

Well, it's always we rambled that river and I
All along your green valley I'll work till I die,
My land I'll defend with my life if it be
'Cause my pastures of plenty must always be free.

—*"Pastures of Plenty," song by Woody Guthrie.*

In September 1965, along the fields of the San Joaquin Valley, up and down the roads bordering grape-growing country throughout the state, crowds of brown-faced men and women appeared carrying red banners with a black eagle on a white circle—symbol of the National Farmworkers' Association. In small, dusty union offices in towns with names like Parlier, Huron, Fresno, La Paz, posters went up: HUELGA! UNIDOS GANAREMOS! (Strike! United We'll Win!) and LA UNION ES NUESTRA FUERZA! (The Union Is Our Strength). The NFWA had joined with the United Farmworkers' Organizing Committee— a union founded by the Filipino farmworker and organizer, Larry Itliong—to launch the great Delano grape strike. The strike was to last five years and catch the whole country up in its energy.

Why was it so important for the farmworkers to form a union? During the time Jessie Lopez De La Cruz was growing up, the average farmworker lived forty-nine years—compared to seventy years for the white majority in the United States. A migrant worker's baby was twice as likely to die as babies of other people. Farmworkers were three times as likely as other people to get tuberculosis, three times as likely to get hurt on the job. They were the lowest-paid workers in the country: on the average, they earned less than two thousand dollars a year.[1]

As for the "farmers" who hired the workers, they hardly fit the typical image of the small family farmer raising a few crops, herding some cows, and feeding chickens. The big California growers had names like Bank of America; Southern Pacific Co.; Times-Mirror Co.; Safeway; Christian Brothers. Farming in California wasn't small. It was, and still is, Big Business—agribusiness.

Farmworkers had tried to organize in the past, but until Cesar Chavez founded the National Farmworkers' Association in 1962, they hadn't been able to form a lasting union. There were several reasons for their failure. The first and most important reason was the tremendous power of the growers and their willingness to use the most violent means of suppressing strikes.[2] The second was that the farmworkers were in great part non-English-speaking people who moved around a lot. It would take organizers who were of the people and who would stay with the people—organizers like the ones who worked for the new union born in 1962—to form an organization that would last. Such efforts had occasionally been made in the past. More often, though, those who tried to organize farmworkers were outsiders, and not farmworkers themselves.

Traditionally, United States trade unions have focused on workplace issues—higher wages, better hours, and improved working conditions. In following this tradition, the earlier farmworkers' organizations made a fatal error. Although on-the-job concerns were very important and continued to be so for the National Farmworkers' Association, so were other issues. The long memories farmworkers had of racism both on and off the job, in every aspect of their lives in the United States, made racial dignity as important a goal as decent wages. Other issues that traditional unions don't consider—for example, farmworkers' ceaseless problems with the United States immigration service—demanded attention.

From its start, the NFWA—which merged with the United Farmworkers' Organizing Committee in 1965 and became the UFW—was unlike other unions. The very fact that it was a union of low-paid, unskilled women and men workers, many of

them black, Chicano, Filipino, and Asian American, was unusual. Cesar Chavez was poor like the people the union organized. He was brown-skinned like them. Like them, he had
very little formal education. Jessie De La Cruz and other organizers came from the same background.

Moreover, the union used very untraditional organizing
methods, some of them coming from deep-rooted Mexican customs. For example, the religious tradition of pilgrimage was the
basis of a three-hundred-mile-long march from Delano to Sacramento, staged by the UFW in March 1966. The pilgrimage called
attention to the farmworkers' plight and to their struggle; it
showed that the Delano grape strike had wide support; and it
lifted the strikers' spirits. It began with eighty people; it passed
through small towns and labor camps. The marchers stayed in
other farmworkers' homes along the way, and often the people
in the towns and camps where they stayed joined the growing
ranks of people walking toward Sacramento. By the time the
pilgrimage reached Sacramento, it had swelled to thousands.
During the march, and largely as a result of it, Schenley Industries, a giant conglomerate, signed a contract—the union's first,
and the first farmworkers had ever had.

Between 1966 and 1967, the union got no other contracts.
Clearly, the strike—the refusal to work and the setting up of
picket lines—was not enough to bring the big growers to the
bargaining table. For this reason, the United Farmworkers
reintroduced the consumer boycott into North American
unionism, urging consumers not to buy at supermarkets that
carried grapes produced by the growers against whom the union
was striking. This boycott, which lasted until 1970, when several major grape growers (including Gallo) signed contracts
with the union, was an international effort. All across the
United States, and in Canada and Scandinavian countries,
where American food products were massively shipped, millions of consumers honored the first grape boycott and a second
grape boycott that followed, as well as a lettuce boycott (1973–
1974).

These extraordinary mass boycotts were made possible by
another highly untraditional method. The union signed up non-

union volunteers—students, clergy, and others—sending them to explain the boycott in front of supermarkets, at church and community meetings. What finally won contracts for the UFW was a combination of the strikes and the boycotts.

As important as these activities was the union's social service work. Without it, the UFW would never have gained the loyalty of the masses of farmworkers. Organizers like Jessie De La Cruz knew from their own lives that off-the-job issues were as important as on-the-job ones. When organizers talked with people about the union, they most often found themselves talking about medical problems, about how to fill out tax forms, about translating a letter or making a phone call in English, about getting support for family problems (child care, death, divorce, an aging relative).[3]

The strikes, the boycotts, the union's social service work— all of these were infused with a special philosophy, one which stressed nonviolence and emphasized racial heritage and dignity. The union also advocated social equality for all poor and working people. The union's philosophy was more than just a lot of words and abstract ideas. It shaped the activities and concerns of the union. For example, before the union existed and won its contracts, Chicano and other farmworkers were prey to the growers' practice of hiring only the youngest and strongest workers. Old workers often were simply laid off—discarded and abandoned to poverty and often to illness. And child labor was rampant. Both the casting-off of the older workers and the overuse of child labor ceased after the union was recognized by company after company.

There were, of course, major problems for the fledgling union. One problem was that it came under continual attack by the growers as well as by some of the United States labor movement's mightiest officials for being *La Causa*—the Cause. These critics said that the UFW was a social protest movement, and not a union at all.

Another problem for the United Farmworkers, as for all beginning unions, was recruiting members. Any new union must have the support of workers who decide that the union will indeed help them. One obstacle to this worker support is fear.

Many employers fight against unionization, telling workers they are better off without a union, that they can be better served by the employers themselves. The growers didn't hesitate to use threats and even brutality against workers who supported the UFW. Nevertheless, despite all of the intimidation, because the UFW *was* unique in its grassroots leadership, in its willingness to help farmworkers in their life problems, and in its almost religious fervor, it gradually gained the wholehearted support of the farmworker majority.*

In their activities—particularly on picket lines—the workers met with a great deal of violence. An unexpected conflict broke out in 1966. Teamster officials began organizing among the farmworkers, too. This was extremely troubling. In the past, the Teamsters—a white-dominated, "outsiders" union—had often acted more in support of the growers than the workers. It was clear that the Teamster officials were quite willing to bend to the will of the big growers more than the UFW was. For example, while the United Farmworkers insisted on stringent rules regarding farmworkers' exposure to pesticides, which had long caused lingering disease and deaths among masses of workers, the Teamsters did not. The UFW insisted on many other health and safety measures that the Teamster officials were willing to forego. Growers preferred the Teamsters, of course, since in the employers' opinion, the fewer concessions they had to make, the better. The Teamster officials hired people—goons—to physically intimidate UFW members and organizers. The Teamsters also red-baited UFW members (called them Communists) and signed contracts with the growers without holding legally-required elections to determine which of the two unions the workers preferred.[4]

In spite of all the hardships,[5] the United Farmworkers won

---

* Once the workers support the union, the next major issue is getting recognition from management—getting the company (in this case, the growers) to agree that the union is the workers official representative. After recognition, the next step is getting a contract. This takes place through collective bargaining—talks between the company and the union representatives, in which the two sides finally come to an agreement on wages, hours, health, safety, and other benefits. When the agreement is reached, it is written up formally in the contract, a document binding to both the company and the workers.

the first contract ever given to farmworkers. That was in 1966, after the Sacramento pilgrimage. During the eleven years that followed, many other contracts were signed.

Cesar Chavez came to visit the De La Cruzes at their house in 1962. It was a "house visit"—Chavez and other organizers routinely spoke with people at home, to talk about what the union was trying to do. Home was where personal contact with workers could be made.[6] It was also a place where the group of people was small enough so that everyone's questions could be answered. Jessie De La Cruz recalls how, listening to Cesar Chavez that evening, she suddenly felt that the Farmworkers' union was a cause for which she had always yearned. Almost immediately she began encouraging other people to join the union. "I'd be chopping cotton and I'd talk about the union to people in rows right next to me." In this way, she became the first woman to organize people in the fields, on the job. Evenings and weekends she began making house visits of her own. She moved people to discuss the way they felt about their treatment on and off the job, and they talked about experiences very much like the ones she has already described in her life.

Like many others, she worked with the union as a volunteer. The UFW was very poor, and many farmworkers earned their money working in the fields while contributing their extra time to the union. By 1967, De La Cruz was known throughout the union as one of its most patient and skilled organizers. In that year, she was made an official organizer, authorized, among other things, to collect union dues. She continued talking to people in the fields and in their homes, while also working in the fields herself. One of her great strengths was bringing together people the growers had long kept hostile to each other. For example, De La Cruz brought the year-round resident workers together with migrant workers, talking with them about the growers' exploitation of both groups. She also brought "green carders"—Mexicans who received a special green permit to work in the United States—into the ranks of the union. Because they were not United States citizens, "green carders" lived under the threat of deportation if they complained about any condition of life or work. If the union was striking a particular grower, that grower could bring "green carders" in to work and so make the strike less effective. It became crucial, therefore, for the United Farmworkers union to organize "green carders," and it was through people like Jessie De La Cruz that it was able to do so.

From 1968 to 1970, De La Cruz was head of the union's hiring hall in Parlier. The "hall" was a small wood house, with the Farmworkers' banner fluttering over it. Having their own union hiring halls was a momentous change for all farmworkers. Before the founding of the UFW, growers had procured workers through *contratistas*—labor contractors. Growers hired the contractors, asking them to scout up as many workers at as cheap a rate as possible. The contractor could be fair-dealing, but more often he was not. Contractors tried to hire only the youngest and the strongest workers, discarding older workers as unfit. They were also ready and eager to hire children along with their parents. Migrant workers were often completely dependent on the *contratista*. In isolated camps, he alone supplied them with—and often charged them exorbitant prices for— food, shelter, transportation to and from the fields and towns. He would buy items and then re-sell them for more than he paid for them, and pocket the difference. Sometimes *contratistas* gratuitously withheld a week's wages from workers. It wasn't uncommon for workers to pay a *contratista* so much of their salaries that they stayed in his constant debt and were consequently his slaves.

This hiring system was one of the first abuses the union attacked. It eliminated labor contractors by doing the hiring itself. In the union hiring hall, cards were kept with the names of union members; in every contract the grower agreed to hire only UFW members. Moreover, the union made a practice of getting the oldest workers hired first. Being in charge of the hiring hall meant keeping track of the filing system; calling workers to tell them where to go to work; being contacted by growers who needed workers. The hiring hall was also a drop-in and meeting center—a place where people came to talk about their off-the-job problems, a place to socialize.

In addition to her office work at the union hiring hall, her work field organizing, and the long, often dangerous hours she spent picketing, Jessie De La Cruz acted as an interpreter in migrant camps around Parlier. She was also called on increasingly to testify at hearings on farm labor and other issues that affected life in the Mexican American community. And she became deeply involved in the kind of community work that distinguished the UFW from other unions. Jessie De La Cruz fought to get food stamps for farmworkers in Fresno. She worked for bilingual education. She was appointed to a host of community and state organizations, including the Fresno County Economic Opportunity Commission, the Central California Action Associates (a community education project in which she taught English to farmworkers), and the state's Commission on the Status of Women. For a time, she taught English on her own television program, beamed at a farmworker audience.

Jessie De La Cruz's growing up, her marriage, her work in the fields, and her childrearing years were not "activist" ones strictly speaking. But they were years of preparation for her political work. Had she not lived the life she did, she would never have been the kind of organizer she is—someone who relates to farmworkers as members of a large family, an organizer of and for the people.

Growing up, I could see all the injustices and I would think, "If only I could do something about it! If only there was somebody who could do something about it! That was always in the back of my mind. And after I was married, I cared about what was going on, but I felt I couldn't do anything. So I went to work, and I came home to clean the house, and I fixed the food for the next day, took care of the children and the next day went back to work. The whole thing over and over again. Politics to me was something foreign, something I didn't know about. I didn't even listen to the news. I didn't read the newspapers hardly at all. *True Romance* was my thing!

(text continued on page 134)

Making History

Jessie Lopez De La Cruz's commitment to organizing farmworkers comes out of a lifetime of working in the fields. Like many other Mexican American activists, she grew up migrating with the crops, living in labor camps, experiencing racism.
1: Supermarket boycott, California.
2: Farmworker doing her family's laundry.
3: Farmworkers' home, Fresno, California, 1961.
4: A member of the United Farmworkers union, with her daughter, picketing a Safeway store in San Francisco, November 1973.
5: Workers going to the fields at 4:00 A.M., Roma, Texas. **6:** Migrants traveling north from Mexico.
7: Working in the fields. **8:** Cesar Chavez during the 300-mile march from Delano to Sacramento, spring 1966.

But then late one night in 1962, there was a knock at the door and there were three men. One of them was Cesar Chavez. And the next thing I knew, they were sitting around our table talking about a union. I made coffee. Arnold had already told me about a union for the farmworkers. He was attending their meetings in Fresno, but I didn't. I'd either stay home or stay outside in the car. But then Cesar said, "The women have to be involved. They're the ones working out in the fields with their husbands. If you can take the women out to the fields, you can certainly take them to meetings." So I sat up straight and said to myself, "*That's* what I want!"

When I became involved with the union, I felt I had to get other women involved. Women have been behind men all the time, always. Just waiting to see what the men decide to do, and tell us what to do. In my sister-in-law and brother-in-law's families, the women do a lot of shouting and cussing and they get slapped around. But that's not standing up for what you believe in. It's just trying to boss and not knowing how. I'd hear them scolding their kids and fighting their husbands and I'd say, "Gosh! Why don't you go after the people that have you living like this? Why don't you go after the growers that have you tired from working out in the fields at low wages and keep us poor all the time? Let's go after them! *They're* the cause of our misery! Then I would say we had to take a part in the things going on around us. "Women can no longer be taken for granted—that we're just going to stay home and do the cooking and cleaning. It's way past the time when our husbands could say, 'You stay home! You have to take care of the children! You have to do as I say!'"

Then some women I spoke to started attending the union meetings, and later they were out on the picket lines.

I think I was made an organizer because in the first place I could relate to the farmworkers, being a lifelong farmworker. I was well-known in the small towns around Fresno. Wherever I went to speak to them, they listened. I told them about how we were excluded from the NLRB in 1935, how we had no benefits, no minimum wage, nothing out in the fields—no restrooms, nothing.* I would talk about how we were paid what the grower wanted to pay us, and how we couldn't set a price on our work. I explained that we could do something about these things by joining a union, by working together. I'd ask people how they felt about these many years they had been working out in the fields, how they had been treated. And then we'd all talk about it. They would say, "I was working for so-and-so, and when I complained about something that happened there, I was fired." I said, "Well! Do you think we should be putting up with this in this modern age? You know, we're not back in the twenties. We can stand up! We can talk back! It's not like when I was a little kid and my grandmother used to say, 'You have to especially respect the Anglos,' 'Yessir,' 'Yes, Ma'am!' That's over. This country is very rich, and we want a share of the money these growers make of our sweat and our work by exploiting us and our children!" I'd have my sign-up book and I'd say, "If anyone wants to become a member of the union, I can make you a member right now." And they'd agree!

So I found out that I could organize them and make members of them. Then I offered to help them, like taking them to the doctor's and translating for them, filling out papers that they needed to fill out, writing their letters for those that couldn't write. A lot of people confided in me. Through the letter-writing, I knew a lot of the problems they were having back home, and they knew they could trust me, that I wouldn't tell anyone else about what I had written or read. So that's why they came to me.

There was a migrant camp in Parlier. And these people, the migrants, were being used as strikebreakers. I had something to do with building that camp. By that time, I had been put on the

* The National Labor Relations Board (NLRB) was established by President Franklin Delano Roosevelt in 1933. Its purpose was to settle differences between employers and employees. The board was set up under the National Labor Relations Act, which made union negotiations between employers and employees legal for the first time in the United States. The act, and the board set up to implement it, were historical landmarks in the history of unionism. But two major groups of workers were excluded by the act and its board—domestic workers (who were mostly women) and farmworkers (who were mainly Chicanos, Filipinos, and blacks). Both major groups were among the poorest of the United States working class.

board of the Fresno County Economic Opportunity Commission, and I was supporting migrant housing for farmworkers. But I had no idea it was going to be turned almost into a concentration camp or prison. The houses were just like matchboxes—square, a room for living, a room for cooking, a bathroom that didn't have a door, just a curtain. The houses are so close together that if one catches fire, the next one does, too, and children have burned in them. It happened in Parlier.

So I went to the camp office and said I wanted to go in and visit. By this time, I was well-known as a radical, an educator, and a troublemaker! The man in the office asked what I wanted to talk about. I just wanted to visit, I said.

"Well, you have to sign your name here." I said, "I also would like to know when I can use the hall for a meeting."

"What kind of meeting?"

"An organizing meeting." You see, when it was built, they told us there was supposed to be a hall built for parties and whatever. I felt we could use it for a meeting to talk to the people. But he said, "We can't authorize you to come in here and talk to the people about a union, but you can write Governor Reagan and ask for permission."* I left.

I met a nurse who had to go to this camp. She said, "Why don't you come with me as my translator?" Even though she spoke perfect Spanish! So both of us went in, and she said she was from the Health Department and I was her translator. I got in there and talked to the people and told them about our union meetings, and at our next meeting they were there. I had to do things like that in order to organize.

It was very hard being a woman organizer. Many of our people my age and older were raised with the old customs in Mexico: where the husband rules, he is king of his house. The wife obeys, and the children, too. So when we first started it was very, very hard. Men gave us the most trouble—neighbors there in Parlier! They were for the union, but they were not taking orders from women, they said. When they formed the ranch committee at

---

* Reagan was the Republican governor of California. A conservative, he was known to be unfriendly to the United Farmworkers.

Christian Brothers—that's a big wine company, part of it is in Parlier—the ranch committee was all men.* We were working under our first contract in Fresno County. The ranch committee had to enforce the contract. If there are any grievances they meet with us and the supervisors. But there were no women on the first committee.

That year, we'd have a union meeting every week. Men, women, and children would come. Women would ask questions and the men would just stand back. I guess they'd say to themselves, "I'll wait for someone to say something before I do." The women were more aggressive than the men. And I'd get up and say, "Let's go on, let's do it!"

When the first contract was up, we talked about there being no women on the ranch committee. I suggested they be on it, and the men went along with this. And so women were elected.

The women took the lead for picketing, and we would talk to the people. It got to the point that we would have to find them, because the men just wouldn't go and they wouldn't take their wives. So we would say, "We're having our picket line at the Safeway in Fresno, and those that don't show up are going to have to pay a five-dollar fine." We couldn't have four or five come to a picket line and have the rest stay home and watch TV. In the end, we had everybody out there.†

One time we were picketing—I think it was the early part of 1972—White River Farms in Delano, for a new contract.[7] To go picket, we had to get up early. See, a lot of these growers were chartering buses, and at four or five o'clock in the morning they'd pick up the scabs. So we would follow these labor bosses who chartered the buses.

---

* On every farm, the union created a ranch committee elected by the workers. The committee is the grassroots base of the union. If you have an on-the-job complaint, you bring it to the ranch committee, which then discusses the complaint with the supervisor. Before the ranch committee was introduced by the union, individual workers had to get up nerve to complain about abuses on their own—and often they were fired on the spot when they dared speak up. The ranch committee put the union behind them and gave them a democratically-elected group for support.

† The picket lines at the Safeway chain were set up to keep consumers from shopping at a store that sold nonunion grapes. The picket lines at the ranches were set up to keep workers from working.

At White River Farms one morning very early, we were out there by the hundreds by the road, and these people got down and started working out there in the grapes. We were asking them not to work, telling them that there was a strike going on. The grower had two guards at the entrance, and there was a helicopter above us. At other White River Farm ranches they had the sheriff, the county police, *everybody*. But there were pickets at three different ranches, and where we were picketing there wasn't anybody except these two guards. So I said, "Hey! What about the women getting together and let's rush 'em!" And they said, "Do you think we could do that?" And I said, "Of course we can! Let's go in there. Let's get 'em out of there any way we can." So about fifty of us rushed. We went under the vines. We had our banners, and you could see them bobbing up and down, up and down, and we'd go under those rows on our knees and roll over. When the scabs saw us coming they took off. All of them went and they got on the bus. The guards had guns that they would shoot, and something black like smoke or teargas would come out. That scared us, but we still kept on. After we saw all those workers get back on the buses, we went back. Instead of running this time, we rolled over and over all the way out. The vines are about four feet tall, and they have wire where you string up the vines. So you can't walk or run across one of these fences. You have to keep going under these wires. So I tripped, and rolled down about three or four rows before I got up. I rolled so they wouldn't get at me when they were shooting. When I got out there on the road they were getting these big, hard dirty clods and throwing them at us. And then the pickets started doing the same thing. When the first police car came, somebody broke the windshield. We don't know if it was the scabs or someone on the picket lines, but the picketers were blamed.

When we women ran into the fields, we knew we'd be arrested if they caught us. But we went in and we told the scabs, "If you're not coming out we're gonna pull you out!" Later I told Arnold, "See? See what women can do? We got all those men out there to come out!"

At another place, in Kern County, we were sprayed with pesticides. They would come out there with their sprayers and spray us on the picket lines. They have these big tanks that are pulled by a tractor with hoses attached, and they spray the trees with this. They are strong like a water hose, but wider. They get it started and spray the vines and the trees. When we were picketing, they came out there to spray the pickets. What could we do? We tried to get as far away as we could, and then we would come back.

They had goons with these big police dogs on leashes. I think they were trying to scare us by letting them loose on us. But those dogs were whining and straining to get loose because they were scared of all the shouting that we were doing! They weren't very brave! We would shout, "Let them go so they can hide! Why put them through this?"

The next year, in '73, we were picketing another ranch in Coachella. That's the first time I saw any of the Teamsters. They were huge. And they had huge rings on their fingers, making gestures at us, and they had clubs. They started singing God Bless America, because they were super-Americans and we were not. They had these big American flags on the backs of their tee-shirts. They said we were nothing, only Chicanos. All we were asking for was recognition of our union. They had dogs. Oh! They were dirty-mouthed people. When the growers realized how strong we were getting and how we had so many members, when our contracts were up for renewal they called the Teamsters in. And even before we bargained for our new contract, the growers signed up with the Teamsters. Then they claimed they already had a union and couldn't recognize ours. That was another way they had of not signing with UFW. They were signing hundreds of what we called "sweetheart contracts."

Another thing the growers did to break our strikes was to bring in "illegal aliens." I would get a list of names of the scabs and give them to the border patrol. At that time, you see, we were pitted against each other, us and the people from Mexico, so it was either us or them. When I went to the border patrol office, I'd go in and say, "Can I come in?" They'd say, "You can't come in. This is a very small office." They kept telling us they were short of men. But every time I went there, there were all of them with their feet up on the desks in their air-conditioned office. They told me they were under orders not to interfere with labor disputes. So I called Bernie Sisk's office and talked to them about it.* Then I came home and called a lot of students who'd been helping us, and other people, and the next morning, there we were at the border patrol. I said, "We're paying our tax money, but not for you to sit here while the illegal aliens are being used to break our strike."

But as I said, we, the strikers, and the illegal aliens were being pitted against each other. And at a hearing in 1973, I told the congressmen, "Our grandparents were illegal aliens once. We've never been against them. We feed them. But you, and you, and you," I pointed at the congressmen, "You Anglos, none of you have more right than these Mexican people here. This land was once Mexico. You came along and built a big fence and said, "You keep on your side of the fence and we'll keep on ours." But you came along and got the *braceros* to use them.† So it's a problem *you* created. They're our blood brothers and blood sisters and you're using them against us!

While I was working for the union, I learned about negotiating for a contract. In 1966, when we were negotiating for a contract with Christian Brothers, Dolores Huerta asked me along.‡ "I want you to learn this because eventually you might have to take over the negotiating of the contracts." I'd sit there at those meetings with the Christian Brothers, who were Catholic priests. Dolores and the ranch committee would argue, "You can't say we're asking for too much money, because just think, you have over fifty varieties of fine grapes that go into making the most expensive wines for the church and they sell at very high prices. So why can't these workers share some of the

---

* Sisk was a Democratic congressman with a reputation of sympathy for farmworkers and small farmers. Later, Sisk turned out far more sympathetic to the big growers.

† Under a program begun in World War II, *braceros* ("hired hands," from the Spanish word, *brazo,* arm), were brought in by the growers to feed their labor needs. The *braceros* were ill-treated and badly paid.

‡ Dolores Huerta, one of the founders of the union, has held key leadership positions in the UFW.

money that comes out of those grapes that they've harvested?" They would bargain back and forth this way. Then the ranch committee would caucus—we would walk out of that meeting room, and we'd drink water and discuss what we were going to say when we went back. We'd say, "They have to meet our demands." We were asking for protective clothing; that they supply the pans we picked the grapes in. We also asked for a smoke device for the tractors. We were on our knees working beside the tractors and we would feel dizzy, smelling all of the smoke from the exhaust pipe for hours. We also didn't have any water on the tractors. To get water we had to go with the tractor driver to where the water was, and then we'd lose time picking and lose money. We demanded that they supply each crew with a can of drinking water, so we could drink water right there when we were thirsty.

Our demands were met, but it was hard bargaining. At one point, one of the Christian Brothers' lawyers said, "Well, sister, it sounds to me like you're asking for the moon for these people." Dolores came back, "Brother, I'm not asking for the moon for the farmworkers. All we want is just a little ray of sunshine for them!" Oh, that sounded beautiful!

In '68, while we were in Parlier, I was put in charge of the hiring hall. My house was right next to the office, and I had an extension to the office phone in my house. I could do the housework and take care of the children, but I could take care of the office, too. Before the contract, the hiring hall was just a union office, where people came to learn about the union. When they got the first contracts, we began dispatching people out to work.

It was up to me to get all the membership cards in order alphabetically. When the grower came to us to ask for workers, I'd look for the ones who were in the union longest, and also working under the Christian Brothers contract. I'd call them: "Can you be ready Monday or Wednesday morning? Be there on time, because you're going to start working for Christian Brothers." One of the things we had to explain over and over to people who had been working for a ranch many years was that no one was going to take their jobs away. The growers told them, "If you sign up for Chavez's union we'll fire you." But the union contract guarantees that the people working here have the right to stay here, so we always made a list of names of people who were working at the ranch. And when the union organizes them, they have the highest seniority, they're the first ones hired.

The hiring hall was also a place where people could meet and talk. A lot of people were migrants who needed to get to know each other. The people who were there all the time were against the migrants. I said, "We have to get these people together. We can't be divided." I was at the hall all day. People would drop by and I'd introduce them.

The second year we had a contract I started working for Christian Brothers. The men were doing the pruning on the grape vines. After they did the pruning, the women's crew would come and tie the vines—that was something we got changed. We made them give pruning jobs to women.

I was made a steward on the women's crew.* If there were any grievances, it was up to me to listen and then enforce the contract. For example, the first time we were paid when I started working, during the break the supervisor would come out there with our checks. It was our fifteen-minute break, which the contract gave us the right to. He always came then! We had to walk to the other end of the row, it took us about five minutes to get there, the rest of the fifteen to get our checks, and walk back, and we'd start working. This happened twice. The third time I said, "We're not going to go after our checks this time. They always come during our break and we don't get to rest." So when we saw the pickup coming with the men who had the checks I said, "Nobody move. You just sit here." I walked over to the pickup. I said to the man inside, "Mr. Rager, these women refuse to come out here on their break time. It's their time to

---

* Every union has its workers elect "shop stewards" from their midst. These officially-elected union representatives remain on the job, working side-by-side with the other employees. Their responsibility is to provide information to their co-workers about the union, and to deal with any complaints—"grievances"—workers may have. The steward is empowered to go to the manager or boss on the workers' behalf, and to consult with other union officials about on-the-job problems.

rest. So we're asking you, if you must come during our rest period, you take the checks to these ladies." From that day on, every payday he would come to us. That was the sort of thing you had to do to enforce the contract.

I became involved in many of the activities in the community—school board meetings, city council meetings, everything that I could get into. For example, I began fighting for bilingual education in Parlier, went to a lot of meetings about it and spoke about it.

You see, when I was a nine-year-old child going to school, I couldn't speak English. I remember vividly one day all the children, mostly Chicanos, were lined up, and we had to stand before this lady all dressed in white, a health nurse. She told me to open my mouth and I just stared at her. She stuck a stick to push my tongue down, and I couldn't help it: I vomited all over her dress. Oh! I started crying, and the teacher came up and she kept saying, "I'm sorry. I'm sorry." Those words stuck to me; I even dreamed them.

Another time something else happened when I ran out of underwear! See, we were very poor, and when I ran out of underwear, grandmother tore open a pillow and used the red satin to make some drawers for me. I was ashamed; I didn't want nobody to see me. I was dressed very different from all the other children in the first place. My dresses were almost down to my ankles and they were gathered in the waist with a drawstring that my grandmother made me, and high boy's shoes and heavy black stockings.

When I got the red underwear, I was out there after school like a little monkey up on the swings and two Anglo girls about my age started teasing me: "Oh, she's got red panties! red panties!" and they tried to lift my dress up. By this time, I was off the swings and standing against the wall. When one of the older girls leaned over to pull my dress up, I lifted my knee and hit her nose and she started bleeding and crying. The teacher came over and she slapped me. But since I didn't know English, I couldn't tell her, I couldn't explain what had happened.

To top it off, being a migrant worker I changed schools about every three to four weeks. As soon as one crop was picked, we went on to the next one. I'd go to school for about a week or two, then I was transferred. Every time we transferred I had a pain in my stomach, I was shaking, scared to go to school.

This is why I began fighting for bilingual education. I didn't want what happened to me to happen to the little children in Parlier whose parents couldn't speak English.

Parlier is over eighty-five percent Chicano, yet during that time there were no Chicanos on the school board, on the police force, nowhere. Now it's changed; we fought to get a Chicano mayor and officials. But then I was asking people, "Why are we always asked to go to the public school for our meetings? Why can't they come over to our side of town in Parlier?" So we began having meetings in *la colonia** at the Headstart Center, and there we pushed for bilingual education.

Fresno County didn't give food stamps to the people—only surplus food.† There were no vegetables, no meat, just staples like whole powdered milk, cheese, butter. At the migrant camp in Parlier, the people were there a month and a half before work started, and since they'd borrowed money to get to California, they didn't have any food. I'd drive them into Fresno to the welfare department and translate for them, and they'd get food, but half of it they didn't eat. We heard about other counties where they had food stamps to go to the store and buy meat and milk and fresh vegetables for the children. So we began talking about getting that in Fresno. Finally, we had Senate hearings at the Convention Center in Fresno. There were hundreds of people listening. A man I know comes to me and says, "Jessie, you're next." He'd been going to speak, but he said he wanted me to speak in his place. I started in Spanish, and the senators were looking at each other, you know, saying, "What's going on?" So then I said, "Now, for the benefit of those who can't

---

* The Chicano neighborhood.
† In 1964, Congress established a program under which low-income people could "pay" for food at stores by using stamps issued by the government. Your eligibility for food stamps depended on your income. When the Welfare office sent you surplus food, you had to eat what you got: you had no choice. But you could take food stamps to your local store, and buy what you wanted.

speak Spanish, I'll translate. They tell us there's no money for food stamps for poor people. But if there is money enough to fight a war in Vietnam, and if there is money enough for Governor Reagan's wife to buy a three-thousand-dollar dress for the Inauguration Ball, there should be money enough to feed these people. The nutrition experts say surplus food is full of vitamins. I've taken a look at that food, this cornmeal, and I've seen them come up and down. But you know, we don't call them vitamins, we call them weevils!" Everybody began laughing and whistling and shouting. In the end, we finally got food stamps for the people in Fresno County.

Sometimes I'd just stop to think: what if our parents had done what we were doing now? My grandparents were poor. They were humble. They never learned to speak English. They felt God meant them to be poor. It was against their religion to fight. I remember there was a huge policeman named Marcos, when I was a child, who used to go around on a horse. My grandmother would say, "Here comes Marcos," and we just grew up thinking, "He's law and order." But during the strikes I stood up to them. They'd come up to arrest me and I'd say, "O.K., here I come if you want. Arrest me!"

Fighting for the Land

We really are the farmers. I know how to plant the grapes. After they grow I know how to prune them. After I prune them I know how to pick them. Millionaires get someone like me doing the work, they don't know what they got.

—*Arnold De La Cruz.*

Organizing for the United Farmworkers, Jessie De La Cruz came to see that improving working conditions and raising wages wasn't enough. So she began talking with other farmworkers about a dream they all shared—buying their own land. In 1972, they formed a committee and went to De La Cruz's old boss, Russell Giffen, who was selling his land on the west side of the valley. Giffen asked for a half-million dollars, and most of the families dropped out of the land struggle, discouraged.

But a sympathizer, Roger McAfee, leased Jessie De La Cruz and her friends six acres of land near Fresno. The cherry tomato crop they planted brought the families sixty-four thousand dollars—enough to buy and improve land several miles away. Four families, the De La Cruzes and three others, bought forty acres and named the land the Rancho El Bracero. For four years, they have worked the land cooperatively, using no pesticides, growing their crops organically, with only a pump and tractors for equipment. The families' ten-acre plots of land have continued reaping enormous yields.[8]

Still, the De La Cruzes and other farmworker families would like to be able to farm on the west side of the valley where Giffen had his land. For the west side—once a desert—contains some of the richest farmland in the world, thanks to a multibillion dollar Federal project that irrigates the parched ground with water from government dams. An act passed in 1902 put the government in charge of paying for the irrigation. The act states that individuals and companies can't own more than 160 acres of land that gets government water. But for the past seventy-five years, growers have evaded the law and have dominated the west side of the San Joaquin Valley. Farmers like Jessie and Arnold De La Cruz have been forced to farm elsewhere. For water, they have had to buy their own pumps and dig their own wells with their own money.

In 1974, Jessie De La Cruz helped found National Land for People, an organization that has been fighting to get the government to enforce the 1902 law and break up the corporate-owned lands so that people like the De La Cruzes can live and farm there. The battle of Emiliano Zapata, Pancho Villa, and the peasant revolutionaries in Mexico at the beginning of the century to break up the big *haciendas* there, echoes in a slogan on a poster that hangs in the National Land for People office in Fresno: THE LAND BELONGS TO THOSE WHO WORK IT!

Jessie De La Cruz now devotes her days to work on the co-op, to the struggle for land ownership, and to speaking around the country about farmworkers' struggles. She is called on to talk at colleges; community meetings; national conferences; and government hearings on food, small family farming, and land redistribution. All the while, the other parts of her life continue. At the vine-covered house in Fresno, there is usually someone visiting in the kitchen—neighbors, children, grandchildren. When she isn't on the farm or at meetings, Jessie De La Cruz is at home—but never without work. She is either at the stove cooking or sitting in conversation, rapidly crocheting or sewing. "I can't be with my hands idle. There is always something to do."

In 1977, at the age of fifty-eight, she returned to school. At the Universidad Libre de Campesinos (Farmworkers' Free University), she took up typing, shorthand, psychology, sociology, history—learning to support the continuing work of a lifetime.[9]

When I was a child, I used to hear my grandfather say, "Someday we'll own a small farm. Even if it's just a house with two or three acres where we can grow some kind of crops. Maybe we'll go back to Mexico and start farming out there." He never had enough money. A lot of people had that dream. If you were around older people talking in an afternoon, they would keep saying, "If I had a farm I would do this, I'd do that. I'd stay in one place"—these were people who migrated—"and build a big house for my family, I'd send them to school so they could get an education." They didn't live long enough to make it a reality.

In 1972, my husband and I got to talking, and then we started having house meetings here in my house. I'd call many people I'd helped organize for the union, and we'd meet and talk about buying maybe twenty-five acres, all the families working together as a co-op. If one family tried it, we thought, we could never make it. If we got a group and were willing to put in what little money everyone managed to save during the grape-picking season or whatever, we could find a farm that we could buy. We continued having the meetings until finally a committee was formed. My husband and I were part of it. We went to Russell Giffen's office; he was supposed to sell his land under the 1902 law. He just asked us, did we have a half-million dollars as downpayment. We just looked at each other and walked out. So then the people became discouraged, saying we'd been given the same runaround as usual.

But six families said they wouldn't give up. And a few weeks later, we heard about a man who had forty acres for sale. It turned out to cost sixteen thousand dollars. I knew we couldn't get land for anything less. We put together what little money each of us had and used that to hold the land until we could raise the money for a downpayment.

The land was piled with tumbleweed that grew taller than I was. There was no water, and there were little hills all over. That winter, in January and February, we had to work cutting the tumbleweed off, burning it, leveling the land. It was raining. We'd go out there and cut the tumbleweed, stack them up high, and burn them.

But we knew we'd have to start planting in March, and we couldn't do this, because the land had to be completely leveled and a well had to be dug. So a man who had been helping us, Roger McAfee, said, "I'll rent you a few acres." On his land, we did the planting on our hands and knees, all the kids and grownups working in March. Sometimes it would go down to twenty degrees. All six families would start in the morning, planting, and work until the night. One night I heard on the radio it was going to be twenty-six degrees. I began crying, "We're going to lose our plants!" I was on my hands and knees that evening, praying and crying and trying to save the tomatoes. I covered them with little tents and then with dirt. The next morning we came back and uncovered them, and they shot up straight as anything!

When we finished picking our crops at the rented place, we ended up with sixty-four thousand dollars—all that from six acres! Of course, we'd worked very hard. We'd done the planting, the picking, the sorting, packing, irrigating, weeding, tying of the vines, everything. We did everything it takes to grow a tomato crop. All of us were there all day long: we still do this on our land now.

By the time we bought our own land, there was only four families left. We sectioned the forty acres into four parts, one for each family. We share machinery—the pumps, the tractors.

We've tried all kinds of crops—bell peppers, zucchini, squash, cucumbers, eggplant, three different varieties of melons, cherry tomatoes, and hot chilies. We've grown a hundred percent organic onions. What we can't sell we give away. How could we say, "We're not going to give this away so the price will go up on tomatoes?" That's what the growers do. If they can't sell, they plow them under or throw them away, because they say, "If I give this away, I won't be able to sell mine at the market."

We kept saying, "What are we going to call ourselves?" At one of the meetings different names came up. One man stood up one evening and he said, "Let's call it Rancho El Bracero. I came here as a wetback.* Then I was taken across the border to Mexico, then I signed up as a *bracero*. As a *bracero* I was mistreated, so I broke my contract with the government, the one I'd signed saying I'd work with the same company wherever they took me to work. And I was on my own, in hiding all the time. . . ."

I knew what he was talking about. In 1944, Arnold and I and the children moved from Giffen's Camp Number Three to a creek, and that's when we first saw the *braceros*. By this time I had three children, Raymond and Junior and Freddy. One day, busloads of men came to the camp. We'd never seen anything like it. They had blue pants and white hats. They came from Mexico. I'd hear them cussing! They were so angry, because they were being fed bad food in the boarding house, which was run by the labor contractor. They got baloney and bread. That's no kind of food for a man that's gonna work ten, twelve hours at hard labor. You can't *do* any work on that. They were so angry they'd just throw the baloney and bread on the rooftops.

Some of the men, including my brothers and Arnold, would talk to them and became friends. We heard stories about Old Mexico, and how they'd been brought out here to work. These *braceros* were mistreated even by our own people, by the labor contractors, who mostly are Chicanos. And by the crew-pushers.

* "Wetback" is a term that describes workers who came across the border without visas—illegally. They were rumored to have gotten across swimming, hence the term "wetback." Actually, they crossed the border by land more often than not.

The labor contractors were in the charge of the camps. The contractor would bring in shirts and pants. If a blue work shirt was two dollars, he'd sell it for four-fifty. A soda that was ten cents, he'd sell for fifteen. He was taking money from the *braceros*.

The *braceros* were cussed at. If they became sick or complained about the food or how hard they were working, the contractor would say, "O.K. You wanna go back to Mexico?" Many of them walked out. They broke the contract. I remember one time we were coming from Cantua to Fresno. There's a long stretch where there are no houses. Just water pumps and long stretches of road. Suddenly, we saw this whole bunch of men walking ahead of us. They were *braceros* coming to Fresno. They'd walked out; they were on their way back to Mexico. At that time there were a lot of coyotes, and if anyone shot one they'd just wrap him over a fencepost. They had these fences on the edge of the road, where the farm came to. And they'd just throw the dead coyote over that. So what these men did, they passed the time piling up skeletons of the coyotes right in the middle of the road, they'd just pass the time, feeling free. They'd put 'em together, and they'd take off again. So because we all had these memories we named our land Rancho El Bracero.

I feel that as long as we're able to work we're going to keep working. If we were able to work for somebody else, we can work our own land. And we will succeed. We might not get rich; we're not looking for that. But at least we'll get enough to say, "O.K., I own my ranch. I feel *proud* of my work." Watch a seed that you put in the ground grow, and take care of it, and harvest that and sell it. Teaching the children to love the land, to love the work, as long as it's theirs. We can't fail. We don't want to buy new cars or anything like that; we wouldn't have any need for them. We're not planning on taking long trips or anything like that!

America was built with small farms. They keep saying that the farmer is the country's backbone. I never heard anything about agribusiness being the backbone of the country, or corporations being the backbone. Just because rich companies came in and took over, does that mean we're going to sit back and watch them and have them dictate to us what we eat?

It doesn't take courage. All it takes is standing up for what you believe in, talking about things that you know are true, things that should be happening, instead of what is happening. That's all it takes. The way I see it, there's more poor people than rich people. We're trying to get together, organize, stick together. Say I'm outside, and something is happening inside my house. I need help, and I shout. They'll probably hear me a couple of houses down. But then other people come with me and I say, "Help me shout so they can hear me downtown." It'll take quite a few people. But if we can get a hundred people together and we all shout at the same time, we'll be heard further, and that's what we're talking about!

About the Authors

ELLEN CANTAROW received her Ph.D. in comparative literature from Harvard University. She has taught American studies and women's studies at a number of colleges, including State University of New York/College at Old Westbury. As a Radcliffe Institute fellow, she studied the labor and women's movements in Italy. Cantarow's many articles on literature and on teaching have appeared in *College English*, *Radical Teacher*, and *Liberation*. She is currently a freelance journalist and a columnist for Boston's *Real Paper*.

SUSAN GUSHEE O'MALLEY teaches literature at Kingsborough Community College/City University of New York. She lived in New Orleans for ten years, where she taught at Louisiana State University and was active in the civil rights movement. O'Malley, who has a Ph.D. in literature from Tulane University, is co-editor of *Radical Teacher*. She and her two children live in Brooklyn, New York.

SHARON HARTMAN STROM teaches women's history at the University of Rhode Island, where she helped develop a women's studies program. Strom, who received her Ph.D. in social history from Cornell University, is currently writing a full-length biography of Florence Luscomb. She lives in Narragansett, Rhode Island, with her husband and three children.

A Note on Language

IN EDITING BOOKS, The Feminist Press attempts to eliminate harmful sex and race bias inherent in the language. In order to retain the authenticity of historical and literary documents, however, our policy is to leave their original language unaltered. We recognize that the task of changing language usage is extremely complex and that it will not be easily accomplished. The process is an ongoing one that we share with many others concerned with the relationship between a humane language and a more humane world.

Notes

Introduction

1. This search to construct a history of women went far beyond a search for women activists who were still living. Teachers in colleges and high schools, graduate students, and others began researching women's history, women's physiology and sexuality, women's writing. So began a mass movement for education reform—Women's Studies.

2. The suffrage movement was much broader in its membership; it did not appeal only to well-to-do women. This is why I stress that it was mainly in cities that women like my grandmother were in the suffrage movement's majority. In rural areas, particularly in the Southwest, farm women were active in the suffrage battle. In some areas, there were also a good many black women active both in suffrage and in the temperance movement. For more information, read the introduction to *The Concise History of Woman Suffrage*, by Mari Jo and Paul Buhle (Urbana: University of Illinois Press, 1978).

3. For more details, read Leo Kanowitz, *Women and the Law: The Unfinished Revolution*, especially chapter 3, "Law and the Married Woman," (Albuquerque: University of New Mexico Press, 1969). For a concise overview of women and the law, see *Rights and Wrongs: Women's Struggle for Legal Equality*, by Susan Cary Nicholas, Alice M. Price, Rachel Rubin (Old Westbury, N.Y.: The Feminist Press, 1979).

4. *Twenty Years at Hull House*, written by Jane Addams in 1910, tells the story of the settlement house movement and of Addams's life (New York: Macmillan, Inc., 1966).

5. Richard O. Boyer and Herbert M. Morais, *Labor's Untold Story* (New York: Banner Press, 1955), p. 186.

6. For the entire song, see *Rebel Voices: An IWW Anthology*, edited by Joyce L. Kornbluh (Ann Arbor: The University of Michigan Press, 1968).

7. The organizing policies of the A F of L were based on sex, race, and national prejudices as well as self-interest. By getting high pay and relatively good working conditions for a minority of the workforce, the A F of L established itself as the organization employers most willingly negotiated with. For employers, it was convenient to keep the masses of labor unorganized and cheap; convenient to concede higher pay and other benefits to a few, rather than having to make mass concessions to a majority. Because of this, employers feared other unions that were trying to organize unskilled workers at the time.

8. Quoted in Sheila Rowbotham, *Women, Resistance, and Revolution* (New York: Pantheon Books, Inc., 1972), p. 111.

9. There were many blacks in large northern cities by the turn of the century, but those who were active in strikes were men. In the first twenty years of this century, black women were denied all but the most menial factory jobs—sweeping floors, cleaning, peeling and processing fruit. For the most part, they worked as farm laborers and as domestic servants. But even black men would not enter the mainstream of the labor movement until the Congress of Industrial Organizations began organizing unskilled and unorganized workers in the thirties.

10. Gerda Lerner, ed., *Black Women in White America* (New York: Random House Vintage, 1973), pp. 8–9.

11. Ibid., p. 199. For further information about Wells, see *Crusade for Justice: The Autobiography of Ida B. Wells* (Chicago: University of Chicago Press, 1970).

12. Lerner, ed., *Black Women*, p. 207. For more information on Terrell and Wells, see *Black Foremothers*, by Dorothy Sterling, which contains biographies of both women (Old Westbury, N.Y.: The Feminist Press, 1979).

13. Murders of black people and attacks on them never entirely disappeared. They came again to national attention in the course of the civil rights movement and black power movement of the sixties, as well as in more recent violence against blacks in the antibusing crusades of the seventies in Boston, Massachusetts, and elsewhere.

14. Gerda Lerner, *The Grimké Sisters from South Carolina: Pioneers for Women's Rights and Abolition* (New York: Schocken Books, Inc., 1971), pp. 161–162.

15. Quoted by Sara Evans, "Women's Consciousness and the Southern Black Movement," in *Southern Exposure*, vol. IV, no. 4 (available from The Feminist Press, Box 334, Old Westbury, NY 11568).

16. Quoted in Rowbotham, *Women, Resistance, and Revolution*, pp. 107–108.

17. It is important to know that black women—including Robinson—did not view themselves in the civil rights movement as white women did. One black woman said that, once South, white women "do all the shit work . . . in a feminine kind of way while [black women] . . . were out in the street battling with the cops. . . . We became Amazons, less than and more

than women at the same time." Relations between black and white women and men were often complicated and filled with tension. For more information, see Evans, "Women's Consciousness and the Southern Black Movement."

18. Beverly Jones and Judith Brown, "Toward a Female Liberation Movement," in *Rebirth of Feminism*, ed. Judith Hole and Ellen Levine (New York: Quadrangle, 1973) p. 111.

19. Stanton to Anthony, December 1, 1853, Theodore Stanton and Harriot Stanton Blatch, eds., *Elizabeth Cady Stanton as Revealed in Her Letters, Diary and Reminiscences.* 2 vols. (New York: Harper & Bros., 1922).

20. For a good introduction to the lives and friendship, see "A Feminist Friendship," in *The Feminist Papers* ed. Alice Rossi (New York: Columbia University Press, 1973), pp. 378–396.

21. The Boston Women's Health Book Collective has recently published a new book on parenting, *Ourselves and Our Children* (New York: Random House, Inc., 1978).

Florence Luscomb

1. From 1900 to 1920, the Socialist party of the United States was a vigorous coalition of farmers, labor organizers, working people, and radical intellectuals who hoped to work through the electoral process to gain socialism. Women formed an important segment of the Party and worked, for instance, in the early struggle to establish birth control clinics. The Socialists succeeded in electing some state legislators and a few city mayors. In 1912, their presidential candidate, Eugene Victor Debs, received nearly 6 percent of the popular vote.

2. Passage of an amendment to the state constitution of Massachusetts requires a two-thirds vote in both houses of two successive legislatures and ratification in a referendum by the voters. By 1915, suffragists had gained enough support to win in the legislature, but still faced opposition from many male citizens and a strong antisuffrage women's movement. Suffragists expected to lose the referendum, and did. All their hard work was really aimed at getting a respectable minority of male votes in the referendum, which they did.

3. The strike in Lawrence, Massachusetts, was launched by a group of Polish women workers in the woolen mills. The Massachusetts state legislature had passed a law, effective January 1, 1912, reducing the work week from fifty-six to fifty-four hours. Workers feared their pay would be cut, and the fears turned out to be justified. On January 11, the Polish women discovered a pay cut in their already meager wages, and walked out of the mill, shouting, "Short pay! Short pay!" The strike that followed swept together in astounding unity more than twenty different ethnic groups and a workforce composed of men, women, and children. Sustained by the radical labor organization, the Industrial Workers of the World, twenty-five thousand workers stayed out of the mills for three months. After weeks of company violence and police brutality, the workers finally won their strike. Pay increases in the strike settlement were offset later by layoffs. But the immediate effect of the strike was to hearten textile workers in other cities for struggles of their own.

4. By the early 1930s, World War I, the "war to end all wars," had become extremely unpopular. Millions had seemingly died in vain.

The League of Nations was breaking down, and countries like Japan, Germany, and Italy were busy building up their armies and annexing new territories. Several exposés by journalists and peace groups revealed the enormous profits made by munitions makers during World War I and the fact that these manufacturers had sold arms to the combatants. In 1934, the Senate endorsed Senator Nye's resolution to investigate the munitions industry. Nye took the resolution's wording from a Women's International League for Peace and Freedom policy statement, which had originally been drafted by Luscomb.

5. Nat Hentoff, *Peace Agitator: The Story of A. J. Muste* (New York: Macmillan, Inc., 1963), p. 74. Muste eventually decided he could not work with Communists and joined the Fellowship of Reconciliation, a peace group which consciously excluded them. One of the reasons for Muste's change of heart was his disillusionment with the tactics of Communists in popular front groups. As Luscomb explains later on in this chapter, the Communists practiced "democratic centralism": the leadership of the Party would decide on a certain policy, discuss it with the membership, and then the membership would carry it out. Leftists outside the Party thought this process did not leave enough room for individual deliberation and group debate. Unlike Muste, however, Luscomb believed that it was still possible to work with Communists, and that excluding them both divided the left and made the Communists victims of red-baiting.

6. Rumors of Joseph Stalin's repressive policies in the Soviet Union were only beginning to reach the United States in the thirties. Later, these rumors were validated, and it turned out that Stalin had sent

thousands of political prisoners in the Soviet Union to remote prison camps. Stalin's policies were publically condemned by the leaders of the Soviet Union and the American Communist Party in 1956. Of course, many liberals and conservatives had an ulterior motive in constantly spotlighting the horrors of Stalinism; they wanted to discredit all leftists by lumping them with Stalin. These tactics were so successful during the fifties that no one on the left could speak up without being labeled a "Stalinist totalitarian" or a "Communist dupe."

7. While the unions honored the no-strike agreement, prices increased more than wages, and after the war there was widespread inflation. Only then did a round of strikes ensue—but the corporations had used the no-strike pledge to gain strength during the war.

8. During the 1930s, the League of Women Voters continued to support government legislation that would benefit working women and consumers. The Women's Party, a group of middle-class and professional feminists, pushed for an Equal Rights Amendment to the Constitution. Since the ERA would erase much of the legislation designed to protect working women, the League of Women Voters opposed it. These two groups spent much of the thirties arguing with each other, and neither attacted any large following from the younger generation of women.

9. Luscomb was called before investigative commissions in New Hampshire and Massachusetts. The Massachusetts commission issued an official report in which it listed the names of those individuals it considered to be, on the basis of conjecture and hearsay, Communists or "fellow-travelers." Luscomb, who was on the list, went to court, arguing that such "blacklisting" was a violation of her civil rights. She won her case.

Ella Baker

1. From the late nineteenth century onward, teaching was one of the only "respectable" occupations for black and white women alike. In general, before World War II, stenography was open to white women but not to black women. Race discrimination decreed that black women would either teach, do domestic work, or do the most menial tasks in factories. In fact, Ella Baker *did* end up teaching in one project—the consumer education drive for which she was hired in the thirties by Roosevelt's Works Progress Administration.

2. The Harlem Renaissance is the name given to a black literary and artistic movement of the twenties. Poets and novelists like Langston Hughes, Zora Neale Hurston, Jean Toomer, Claude McKay, searched for the origins and essence of black experience. They were creating new ways of seeing themselves and the communities from which they had come and were rejecting white standards of beauty, speech, and ways of acting. They wrote about black life in the rural South and ghettos of the North. They wrote of Africa and its traditions. They constituted, as a group, the first black pride movement among artists and intellectuals.

3. Ella Baker also had other reasons for resigning from the National Association for the Advancement of Colored People. In her letter of resignation, she stated that the organization was falling short of its real possibilities and that objective and honest discussion within the organization did not seem likely at the time.

4. The decision was based on a suit brought by a black man, Plessy, against a white man, Ferguson, who had tried to make Plessy leave an all-white railroad coach in Louisiana. Louisiana had just passed one of the nation's first state segregation laws. When Plessy refused to leave, he was arrested. He challenged the constitutionality of the arrest, and in the case, "Plessy versus Ferguson," the Supreme Court ruled against him. Not until 1954 did the Supreme Court rule partially against segregation by declaring it illegal in public schools. It was Plessy's ancestor-in-protest, Rosa Parks, who began the landslide that was finally to end all *legal* segregation.

5. This explanation of nonviolent civil disobedience is based on Howard Zinn's, in his book *SNCC: The New Abolitionists* (Boston: Beacon Press, 1964).

6. The Democratic party offered a compromise position which was rejected by the Mississippi Freedom Democratic Party. They would seat Aaron Henry, the head of the NAACP in Mississippi, and Ed King, a Mississippi-born white minister at Tougaloo College, as delegates-at-large; the regular, all-white Mississippi delegation would be seated if they agreed to support the national ticket in the upcoming election.

Jessie Lopez De La Cruz

1. Elizabeth Sutherland Martinez and Enriqueta Longeaux y Vasquez, *Viva la Raza!* (New York: Doubleday & Co., Inc., 1974), p. 189.

2. "For several years," write Martinez and Vasquez of organizing in the 1930s, "it was like wartime in California. When two thousand workers struck in the celery fields, tear-gas bombs were thrown into shacks where the workers' children were playing. One striker was seriously wounded by a tear-gas bomb fired at close range. Many of the people hurt weren't even on strike." (*Viva la Raza!*, p. 130.) In the history of farmworker organizing, before and after the 1930s, and during the struggles of Chavez's union, there have been countless examples of growers' brutality against workers trying to unionize.

3. Ann Witthorn has written about the United Farmworkers' service work in *Radical America*, vol. 12, no. 4 (Summer 1978). I am grateful to her for letting me read a chapter from her unpublished doctoral thesis, which describes the union's service work in great detail.

4. The winter of 1975–76 would later prove that the UFW was the union the workers preferred. It won twice as many elections as the Teamsters, covering over forty thousand workers. The Teamsters and the UFW finally signed a pact in March 1977. The Teamsters withdrew from the fields. The UFW agreed to honor traditional Teamster turf in canneries, cooling plants, loading places, etc. An interesting aspect of the Teamster issue was that across the country, certain Teamster rank-and-file workers rebelled against their officials, supporting the farmworkers. One of the reasons the Teamsters ultimately gave up trying to organize farmworkers was because of restiveness within its own ranks.

5. One of these hardships was that the grape and lettuce growers, giant corporations linked with supermarket chains—Safeway, for example—had the cooperation of some powerful government agencies. For instance, in 1969 the UFW disclosed that over the four years since the grape strike had begun, the De-

fense Department had increased its grape buying by seven hundred percent.

6. House visits are a traditional union organizing technique, but they had not been common in farmworker organizing until the United Farmworkers' union of the 1960s was formed. The reason was that most earlier organizers had come from outside the farmworkers' community; many of them couldn't speak Spanish; they didn't know community customs. And so they usually restricted themselves to speaking with workers either as they were leaving work, or as they were getting into buses in the early morning to go to the fields.

7. White River Farms was a new name given to property formerly owned by Schenley Industries. Schenley sold the properties to Buttes Gas and Oil, an expanding agribusiness conglomerate. The union contract with Schenley had been the farmworkers' first victory. Signed in 1966 and renegotiated in 1969, the contract was due to expire in June 1972. Buttes Gas and Oil was uncooperative in renegotiating the 1972 contract; the UFW called the strike. The White River Farms action was more than just a local strike, for it triggered massive reactions from the Nixon administration that revealed the administration's antilabor attitudes. For more details on what labor reporter Ronald B. Taylor has

called "one of the largest antilabor conspiracies ever assembled," read Taylor's *Chavez and the Farmworkers* (Boston: Beacon Press, 1975), pp. 288–290.

8. Jessie De La Cruz and the others contend that small-family farming can produce as much as agribusiness can, and with less waste. Ever since the 1930s, the government has paid agribusiness *not* to plant, or to give surplus crops to the government, and so keep large parts of the crops off the market. Underproducing, or keeping what is produced out of stores and supermarkets, guarantees that food prices will stay high. Letting land go to waste, or deliberately keeping food off the market, is good for agribusiness prices. But it isn't good for consumers, who wind up paying more for less. Another waste in United States agribusiness is the money spent on costly machinery and chemicals. Research has shown that much of the sophisticated technology now used in agribusiness is not needed to get plentiful crops.

9. The school was founded in 1972 under the auspices of the Greater California Education Project, a federally-funded organization interested in continuing education for farmworkers. The Universidad Libre de Campesinos closed in April 1978 for lack of funds. Some of the faculty and students are now trying to revive a similar college for Chicanas.

Bibliography

Florence Luscomb:
For Suffrage, Labor, and Peace

Note: Statements by Florence Luscomb that appear in this book were taken from interviews and speeches recorded in 1972 and 1973 by Sharon Strom and Steven Halpern. The original tapes and transcripts are in the Oral History Project of the University of Rhode Island.

OVERVIEWS OF RADICAL POLITICS

DIGGINS, JOHN P. *The American Left in the Twentieth Century.* New York: Harcourt Brace Jovanovich, 1973.

WEINSTEIN, JAMES. *Ambiguous Legacy: The Left in American Politics.* New York: New Viewpoints, 1975.

OVERVIEWS OF WOMEN'S HISTORY

BANNER, LOIS. *Women in Modern America.* New York: Harcourt Brace Jovanovich, 1974.

BAXANDALL, ROSALYN; GORDON, LINDA; and REVERBY, SUSAN. *America's Working Women.* New York: Random House, 1976.

PEACE AND CIVIL LIBERTIES

REITMAN, ALAN, ed. *The Pulse of Freedom.* New York: W. W. Norton & Co., 1975.

WITTNER, LAWRENCE S. *Rebels Against War: The American Peace Movement, 1941–1960.* New York: Columbia University Press, 1969.

EARLY WOMEN'S RIGHTS MOVEMENT

BUHLE, MARI JO, and BUHLE, PAUL, eds. *The Concise History of Woman Suffrage.* Urbana: University of Illinois Press, 1978.

CHAMBERS, CLARKE A. *Seedtime of Reform: American Social Service and Social Action.* Minneapolis: University of Minnesota Press, 1963.

FLEXNER, ELEANOR. *Century of Struggle: The Woman's Rights Movement in the United States.* New York: Atheneum, 1970.

LEMONS, J. STANLEY. *The Woman Citizen: Social Feminism in the 1920s.* Urbana: University of Illinois Press, 1973.

O'NEILL, WILLIAM L. *The Woman Movement: Feminism in the United States and England.* New York: Barnes and Noble, 1969.

EARLY SOCIALIST PARTY

GINGER, RAY. *Eugene V. Debs: The Making of an American Radical.* New York: Collier, 1962.

WEINSTEIN, JAMES. *The Decline of Socialism in America, 1912–1925.* New York: Monthly Review Press, 1967.

LABOR STRUGGLES

BERNSTEIN, IRVING. *Turbulent Years: A History of the American Worker, 1933–1941.* Boston: Houghton Mifflin, 1970.

FLYNN, ELIZABETH GURLEY. *The Rebel Girl.* New York: International Publishers, 1973.

LYND, ALICE, and LYND, STAUGHTON. *Rank and File: Personal Histories by Working Class Organizers.* Boston: Beacon Press, 1973.

SIMON, RITA JAMES. *As We Saw the Thirties: Essays on Social and Political Movements of a Decade.* Urbana: University of Illinois Press, 1967.

POSTWAR AMERICA

BELFRAGE, CEDRIC. *The American Inquisition.* Indianapolis: Bobbs Merrill, 1973.

GRIFFITH, ROBERT, and THEOHARIS, ALAN. *The Specter: Original Essays on the Cold War and the Origins of McCarthyism.* New York: New Viewpoints, 1974.

LaFeber, Walter. *America, Russia, and the Cold War, 1945–1966.* New York: John Wiley & Sons, 1968.

Markowitz, Norman D. *The Rise and Fall of the People's Century: Henry A. Wallace and American Liberalism, 1941–1948.* New York: Free Press, 1973.

THE SIXTIES AND SEVENTIES

Cohen, Michael, ed. *The New Student Left: An Anthology.* Boston: Beacon Press, 1967.

Hole, Judith, and Levine, Ellen. *Rebirth of Feminism.* New York: Quadrangle, 1971.

Horowitz, David. *The Free World Collosus: A Critique of American Foreign Policy in the Cold War.* New York: Hill & Wang, 1965.

Ella Baker:
Organizing for Civil Rights

GENERAL BACKGROUND
IN BLACK HISTORY

Aptheker, Herbert, ed. *A Documentary History of the Negro People in the United States.* New York: Citadel, 1951.

DuBois, W. E. B. *The Souls of Black Folk.* New York: Fawcett-World, 1976.

Franklin, John Hope. *From Slavery to Freedom: A History of Negro Americans in the United States.* New York; Alfred A. Knopf, 1947.

Harris, Middleton, et al. *Black Book.* New York: Random House, 1973.

Lerner, Gerda. *Black Women in White America: A Documentary History.* New York: Vintage, 1973. (The single best introduction to Black women in U.S. history, this also has an excellent bibliography.)

SLAVERY AND ABOLITION

Bayliss, John F., ed. *Black Slave Narratives.* New York: Macmillan, 1970.

Brent, Linda. *Incidents in the Life of a Slave Girl.* Edited by L. Maria Child. New York: Harcourt Brace Jovanovich, 1973.

Douglass, Frederick. *Narrative of the Life of Frederick Douglass, An American Slave.* New York: New American Library, 1968.

THE DEPRESSION

Boyer, Richard O., and Morais, Herbert M. *Labor's Untold Story.* New York: Banner Press, 1955.

Salzman, Jack, ed. *Years of Protest.* New York: Pegasus, 1967.

Terkel, Studs. *Hard Times: An Oral History of the Great Depression.* New York: Avon Books, 1970.

GENERAL WORKS ON THE
CIVIL RIGHTS MOVEMENT

Belfrage, Sally. *Freedom Summer.* New York: Viking, 1968.

Bennett, Lerone Jr. *What Manner of Man: Martin Luther King, Jr.* Chicago: Johnson Publishing Co., 1964.

Hansberry, Lorraine, ed. *The Movement: Documentary of a Struggle for Equality.* New York: Simon and Schuster, 1964. (Photographic history.)

Southern Exposure. Vol. IV, no. 3, *On Jordan's Stormy Banks: Religion in the South* and vol. IV, no. 4, *Generations: Women in the South.* (Both issues of the journal are available from *Southern Exposure* P.O. Box 230, Chapel Hill, N.C. 27514.)

Sutherland, Elizabeth, ed. *Letters from Mississippi.* New York: McGraw-Hill, 1965.

Walker, Alice. *Meridian.* New York: Harcourt Brace Jovanovich, 1976. (Novel.)

Zinn, Howard. *SNCC: The New Abolitionists.* Boston: Beacon Press, 1965.

**AUTOBIOGRAPHICAL ACCOUNTS
OF THE CIVIL RIGHTS MOVEMENT**

BATES, DAISY. *The Long Shadow of Little Rock: A Memoir.* New York: David McKay, 1962.

FORMAN, JAMES. *The Making of Black Revolutionaries: A Memoir.* New York: Macmillan, 1972.

MOODY, ANNE. *Coming of Age in Mississippi.* New York: Dial Press, 1968. (The best single introduction to what it was like to be a black student participant in the civil rights movement.)

Jessie Lopez De La Cruz: The Battle for Farmworkers' Rights

Note: Almost every book on Mexican Americans, including all but two (*Salt of the Earth* and *Viva la Raza*) listed below, either emphasizes the experience of Chicano males or entirely leaves out that of women and girls. The study of Chicanas is relatively new, and there is, for example, no Chicana counterpart to Gerda Lerner's *Black Women in White America.*

GENERAL BACKGROUND ON MEXICO

RUSSELL, PHILIP. *Mexico in Transition.* Austin, Tex.: Colorado River Press, 1977.

WOLF, ERIC. *Sons of the Shaking Earth.* Chicago: University of Chicago Press, 1959.

**THE MEXICAN AMERICAN
EXPERIENCE**

ACUÑA, RUDY. *A Mexican American Chronicle.* New York: Americano Book Co., 1971. (Excellent for students and general readers.)

GALARZA, ERNESTO. *Merchants of Labor: The Mexican Bracero Story.* San Jose, Calif.: The Rosicrusian Press, 1965.

LUDWIG, ED, and SANTIBAÑEZ, JAMES. *The Chicanos: Mexican American Voices.* New York: Penguin, 1977. (Includes fiction and nonfiction.)

MARTINEZ, ELIZABETH SUTHERLAND, and LONGEAUX Y VASQUEZ, ENRIQUETA. *Viva la Raza.* New York: Doubleday & Co., 1974.

MCWILLIAMS, CAREY. *North from Mexico: The Spanish-Speaking People of the United States.* New York: J. B. Lippincott Co., 1949.

MEIER, MATT S., and RIVERA, FELICIANO. *The Chicanos: A History of Mexican Americans.* New York: Hill and Wang, 1972. (Includes a very useful bibliography.)

STEINER, STAN. *La Raza: The Mexican American.* New York: Harper & Row, 1969.

**CESAR CHAVEZ AND THE
FARMWORKERS' MOVEMENT**

DAY, MARK. *Forty Acres: Cesar Chavez and the Farm Workers.* New York: Praeger, 1971.

LEVY, JACQUES E. *Cesar Chavez: Autobiography of La Causa.* New York: W. W. Norton & Co., 1975.

LONDON, JOAN, and ANDERSON, HENRY. *So Shall Ye Reap.* New York: Thomas Y. Crowell Co., 1970.

MATTHIESEN, PETER. *Sal Si Puedes: Cesar Chavez and the New American Revolution.* New York: Dell Publishing Co., 1973.

NELSON, EUGENE. *Huelga.* Delano, Calif.: Farmworkers Press, 1966.

FICTION AND DRAMA

NELSON, EUGENE. *The Bracero.* Berkeley, Calif.: Thorp Springs Press, 1972.

WILSON, MICHAEL. *Salt of the Earth.* Commentary by Deborah Silverton Rosenfelt. Old Westbury, N.Y.: The Feminist Press, 1978. (An excellent work, readily accessible to high school and college students and general readers, on Mexican American women and their role in an historic strike.)

Index

The numbers in italics indicate pages with illustrations.

Photograph Acknowledgments

Cover: Brown Brothers. *Page iv:* © by Diana Davies. *Pages 2–3:* Brown Brothers. *Pages 52–53:* Bruce Davidson, Magnum Photos. *Pages 94–95:* © by George Ballis, National Land for People.

Pages 18–19: Florence Luscomb. **Far right:** Brown Brothers. **1:** The Schlesinger Library, Radcliffe College. **2:** *Boston Globe.* **3:** courtesy of Florence Luscomb. **4:** courtesy of the personal papers of Florence Luscomb. **5:** Eric Roth, The Picture Cube. **6, 7:** © by Steven Halpern. **8:** courtesy of Florence Luscomb.

Pages 36–39: Making History. **1, 2:** Brown Brothers. **3:** Culver Pictures. **4:** Brown Brothers. **5:** The Schlesinger Library, Radcliffe College. **6:** Brown Brothers. **7:** Eric Roth, The Picture Cube. **8:** © 1978 by Diana Mara Henry.

Pages 66–67: Ella Baker. **Far right:** courtesy of Anne Braden. **1, 2, 3:** courtesy of Ella Baker. **4:** *Southern Patriot,* courtesy of Anne Braden. **5:** courtesy of Ella Baker. **6:** Wide World Photos. **7:** © by Doug Harris. **8:** © by Sylvia Plachy.

Pages 78–81: Making History. **1:** Culver Pictures. **2:** Bob Adelman, Magnum Photos. **3:** Rufus Hinton, courtesy of Anne Braden. **4:** *The Crisis,* 1932; courtesy of Moorland-Spingarn Research Center. **5:** Norris McNamara, Nancy Palmer Photo Agency. **6:** Bruce Davidson, Magnum Photos. **7:** *Ebony* Magazine. **8:** © by Dick Read.

Pages 112–113: Jessie Lopez De La Cruz. **Far right, 1:** courtesy of Jessie De La Cruz. **2:** © by George Ballis, National Land for People. **3, 4:** courtesy of Jessie De La Cruz. **5, 6, 7, 8:** © by George Ballis, National Land for People.

Pages 130–133: Making History. **1, 2, 3:** © by George Ballis, National Land for People. **4:** Howard Detrick, Nancy Palmer Photo Agency. **5:** © by George Ballis, National Land for People. **6:** Brown Brothers. **7:** Paul Fusco, Magnum Photos. **8:** © by George Ballis, National Land for People.

This book was composed on the VIP in Trump and Olive Antique by Monotype Composition Company, Baltimore, Maryland. It was printed and bound by R. R. Donnelley & Sons Company, Chicago, Illinois. The covers were printed by Algen Press, Queens, New York.